"Austyn Wells is both a teacher and student of life in her practice as well as this book. In order to help raise YOUR awareness, she shares her journey, abilities, and insights. *Soul Conversations* is a guide for living an intuitive life."

—**John Edward**, psychic medium

"In a world that is drowning in information yet hungering for genuine wisdom, Austyn Wells's remarkable book *Soul Conversations* emerges as a guiding light from a higher perspective to show us the way back to meaning, balance, and connectedness in our lives. Having seen far beyond the scope of the human mind and explored realms that most of us cannot imagine, Austyn teaches us how to recognize and nurture our own Souls so that we can live with greater purpose, courage, and love. Through compelling stories of communication beyond the physical plane, descriptions of the energetic tools available to us, thoughtful writing exercises, and illuminating guided meditations, *Soul Conversations* offers a unique curriculum for spiritual evolution that is both profound and simple in its clarity. If you long to connect with a loved one who has died, to know the essence of your own True Nature, to find the purpose for your earthly existence, or to expand your consciousness, *Soul Conversations* can guide you on your journey and provide you with insight and inspiration. This highly recommended book should be both the first and the last text you read as you travel through this human existence."

—**Karen M. Wyatt, MD**, hospice physician, spiritual teacher, speaker, and author of the award-winning *What Really Matters*

"I have followed Austyn's work for years, and am delighted to see that her wisdom and insight will now reach more people by way of this beautiful book. She is a truly inspired teacher with extraordinary skills; deep, heartfelt compassion; and the highest possible integrity. The book is a must-read for anybody interested in the soul's journey."

—**Rev. Terri Daniel, MA, CT**, certified in death, dying, and bereavement; founder of the Association for Death Education and Counseling (ADEC) and The Afterlife Conference

"Medium, mystic, healer, and shaman Austyn Wells shares her knowledge and opens her heart so you can have a conversation with your soul, and walk your own unique and powerful path with grace and ease. You will LOVE this simple and clear, yet in-depth road map to exploring your soul! You will learn something new, resonate with her stories, be pushed and gently prodded, and be inspired and touched. *Soul Conversations* is a must-read for anyone who wants to dance with miracles and magic, deeply contribute to this world, and know the love of their own soul."

—**Linda L. Fitch**, internationally recognized shaman, teacher, and coach; former CEO of the Four Winds Society and dean of its Light Body School of Energy Medicine

"Austyn Wells's book *Soul Conversations* contains well-researched historical information, dynamic use of comparative mythology, probative and revealing personal experiences, effective and simple exercises, and a complete look at all paths available—all with the cardinal merit of clarity."

—**David Hinshaw**, president of Life After Life Institute, and documentary filmmaker

"Austyn's book goes beyond mediumship and inspires each of us to explore the deeper calling of our soul. She serves as a sage teacher, showing us how to bring forth the wisdom that resides within our timeless selves. Austyn invites each of us to take responsibility through boldly offering our unique gifts and, in so doing, manifesting a kinder and more just world for all beings."

—**William Peters, MEd, MFT**, founder of Shared Crossing Project, and director of Shared Crossing Research Initiative

"Austyn has written a wonderfully informative book that answers so many questions regarding the soul, Spirit, and life journeys. The author cogently discusses the many ways we can open our hearts and minds to connect with our own inner self. Those who have questions about death and the soul will find the answers in a way that only Austyn can explain. A must-read for anyone on a spiritual journey."

—**Suzane Northrop**, medium, and author of
Everything Happens for a Reason

"*Soul Conversations* provides a great base for spirituality that comes from the heart. The exercises are practical and are of a form that will help you access your insight—of yourself and psychic and spirit perceptions."

—**Loyd Auerbach**, president of Forever Family Foundation, and parapsychologist

"Austyn Wells has written a must-read book for anyone considering deepening their own spiritual connection. It is a great guide with soulful information taking you on a true spiritual journey. Austyn is a compassionate and honest colleague I highly recommend. Read this book—and learn from one of the best in our field."

—**A.J. Barrera**, psychic medium, intuitive counselor, and intuitive investigator

"*Soul Conversations* will help heal your heart and inspire you to discover your true potential so you can live a soul-centered life."

—**Christine Silver**, affiliate leader of Healing Parents Heal, Ventura County Chapter

"*Soul Conversations* is an awe-inspiring, soulful guide to assist anyone yearning to deepen their ability to listen to the infinite wisdom of their soul, and connect to their loved ones and guides in spirit."

—**Barbara Bartolome**, founder and director of the International Association for Near-Death Studies (IANDS), Santa Barbara, CA

"The only thing harder than losing a child, as I did, is losing the hope that one will ever see that child again. Since first meeting Austyn, and having ever so carefully vetted her abilities, she has helped many of our Grief Haven parents, spouses, siblings, and others who have lost someone they love so dearly that they thought they would lose their minds. One thing they all had in common after meeting Austyn: hope. Even the naysayers were changed. Austyn soars into our hearts, homes, and brains as her gift of immortality with our loved ones gives us hope. She is the Master of Endless Possibilities. *Soul Conversations* is a gift of a book that becomes an earthly guide, a compass that shows us that by being connected with our loved ones, we can live more soul-centered lives— lives that are lived from the perspective of gratitude and remembrance of who we truly are."

—**Susan Whitmore**, founder and CEO of Grief Haven

"Austyn's work in the world is like no other. This book is a glorious reflection of that—her God-given talent, experience, study, and wisdom. Part of her work as a 'validator' (medium) shows us that we all continue after death and we can connect with our loved ones. That in itself is inspiring. Though the greater gift of this book for me is how Austyn lovingly escorts us back to ourselves—to recognize and regain the knowledge of our unlimited beauty and potential, longing to birth into the world. Most of us have forgotten that. She validates again that all of those inklings and nudges that seem to have no solid place in this 3-D reality are the 'real us,' and are given their rightful place and acknowl- edgment. This book is delicious and a delight to revisit, which is why it is my new bedside book. What an amazing guide to uncover your personal holographic landscape—the scenery is fantastic!"

—**Patty Burgess**, cohost of the YouTube show
   The Death Chicks, end-of-life/hospice educator,
   EOL doula trainer, and possibility thinker

SOUL
CONVERSATIONS

A Medium Reveals

How to Cultivate Your Intuition,

Heal Your Heart,

and Connect with the Divine

AUSTYN WELLS

REVEAL PRESS

AN IMPRINT OF NEW HARBINGER PUBLICATIONS

Publisher's Note

Distributed in Canada by Raincoast Books

Copyright © 2019 by Austyn Wells
        Reveal Press
        An imprint of New Harbinger Publications, Inc.
        5674 Shattuck Avenue
        Oakland, CA 94609
        www.newharbinger.com

Cover design by Amy Shoup

Acquired by Catharine Meyers

Edited by Melanie Bell

Illustrations by Marissa Pastor

All Rights Reserved

Library of Congress Cataloging-in-Publication Data on file

21   20   19

10   9   8   7   6   5   4   3   2   1   First Printing

To my mom
Thank you for bringing me into this world
and teaching me the power of soul conversations.
By your being you,
I became the best me.

Contents

Foreword

We are connected to an infinite intelligence some call spirit, source, All, or God. There is a circle of love that includes all living souls and all souls who are in spirit; it includes our lives in the physical world and in the nonphysical domain that souls inhabit between incarnations. The curtain of death appears to separate these worlds—but this is just illusion, an artifact of the amnesia we experience at birth. Because our past lives are forgotten, and our life in spirit is merely a belief, we live on this planet with no idea of how to connect to the spirit world.

Soul Conversations pulls back the curtain between life and death, and shows how to enter the circle of love that holds all souls—embodied and in spirit. This is the first book to show how anyone—not just a medium, shaman, or psychic—can connect directly to the spirit world. You don't have to be an oracle to hear from the other side. There are senses in every soul that you can tune to the voice of spirit. Austyn Wells reveals how to use soul senses to access your own spiritual knowledge, as well as voices far beyond our physical realm. The path for connecting to spirit requires skills—finding our own wisdom, listening within, using our soul senses, and attuning to the Spirit (our own spiritual essence, souls on the other side, guides, and the divine guidance from *All*).

This book will show you how to recognize the voice of Spirit inside you. And how to listen to the voices of love and support, invisible yet powerful, that are all around you. Just as we can learn mindfulness to discover that we have an *awareness beyond our minds*, Austyn Wells shows that we possess the ability to use *soul senses* to access our own intuitive truth and the nature of the spirit world.

I am a psychologist and researcher. And I believe in science. But I also know that the invisible world of spirit has enormous influence on human experience and well-being. Feeling cut off from Spirit, from the circle of love, leaves us feeling alone, afraid, and alienated. Without a relationship to Spirit we are left only to seek pleasure and avoid pain. We struggle with no clear sense of purpose or connection.

Your soul, and every soul you've ever loved, has an infinite light. And that light, that love, connects and guides us. It is the channel through which we speak and listen—to each other, to *All*, and to the divine. *Soul Conversations* reveals the secrets of mediums, shamans, and sages who know how to open this channel. It gives you the power to do what they have done—talk to Spirit, listen to Spirit, be guided by Spirit.

Begin the process now. Reclaim your place in the circle. Start the conversation that will liberate you from loss and fear, and help you hear the support and love that's all around you.

—Matthew McKay, Ph.D.
Author of *Seeking Jordan*
Co-author of *The New Happiness*

Acknowledgments

Books do not happen suddenly. They exist within you. For them to be birthed, the author needs love, support, and incredible fearlessness to overcome the doubt that emerges. Therefore, I must recognize the invisible and visible participants who helped me walk the path to allow *Soul Conversations* to emerge.

My spiritually powerful paternal grandmother, Net, told me she would be more available to me after she died. My spiritual mom, Sally Kienitz, healed my heart and inspired my discovery of tarot. Robin Charin, a Los Angeles party planner, scheduled me for a party as a tarot reader before I felt I was ready, saying "Just keep talking and smile—you will be fine." Event planner extraordinaire Debbie Geller trusted me with her gazillion high-end clients and made me feel like her family. Frank Lucero at Universal Studios connected me to Maritz and Toyota. At Maritz, Butch Noland hired me and let me participate in the AST Dew and NBA Jam Tours so the spirit world could really come crashing in.

John Edward, thank you for walking with me and being so integral. I honor your insight and will never have the words to express the fullness of my gratitude for inviting me to join InfiniteQuest.

Robert Brown trusted me and invited me to Edgar Cayce's Association for Research and Enlightenment for his annual Spiritual Retreat. Your heart and deep commitment to our work renders me speechless.

To the indelible Suzane Northrop, thank you for your friendship.

The loss of a child can inspire tremendous courage and drive within a parent. Thank you to contributing mothers Deanna and Mary for your courage and truth. Lydia, thanks for not only contributing, but guiding me in the final stages of this book. Danny's entrance into the spirit world inspired Terri Daniel to create the Afterlife Conference for which I am now a board member. Terri, thank you for getting all of me and helping me fly.

In my shamanic studies, thank you to Linda Fitch, my *pachamama*, for being my mountain.

This book would not have been created without the love and dedication of the staff at New Harbinger. So many meetings and hours were put into making *Soul Conversations* possible. Thank you to marketing and advertising for shaping the subtitle and Cassie for the superlotto jackpot final title. Thank you, Amy for the cover art and Michele for shaping the illustrations. Julie and Lisa, thanks for truly getting what my book was promising. I found my author voice with the help of Jennifer Holder and Clancy Drake. Cheers to Melanie Bell for copyediting *Soul Conversations* and offering such great insight.

Jordan, thank you for trusting me to tell your dad about the book you wrote together. I know your dad and mom look for your presence in this world every day. I have been honored, Matt, to be included in *Seeking Jordan*. Thank you for cheering me on this journey.

Catharine, my new lifer pal, you are the single reason I am an author. To have a publisher who believes in you is a gift all by itself, but your encouragement and trust has given me wings. May we always fly together.

Marissa Pastor, thank you for your talent and flexibility to draw another kind of universe.

To my husband, Justin, for knowing who I was before I did and not thinking any of this is weird. Thanks, bestie Jane, for being forever Dory and saying just the right thing at the right time. To my soul sista Heather for being constantly inspiring and pushing my limits to help me find more within myself. To my soul brother, medium Chris Drew, for being a true friend and someone I cannot wait to see fly higher.

I would not be writing this if it were not for my clients. Thank you for trusting me with your families, friends, and pets. To the invisible world for letting me speak on your behalf. To my spiritual family, footed and furred, especially Pastor Judy and Kahea.

Finally, to my dad. I know you have been part of this journey. I miss you every day. Thanks for all the ways you still make me feel like the luckiest daughter alive.

Introduction

In ancient Egypt, the heart was seen as part of the soul. Unlike the rest of the organs, the heart remained within the body when a person was mummified. The ancient Egyptians believed that in order to enter the afterlife, all souls were judged on how they lived. To determine this integrity, a soul's heart was placed upon a large scale and weighed against the ostrich feather of Maat, the goddess of cosmic order. If the heart weighed the same as the feather, that soul had lived a true and just life.

If you weighed your heart against a feather, how would you do? I ask this because the only way to shift how we live is by living from our soul and allowing all of our exchanges to be soul conversations.

I have always believed that each person upon this earth is miraculous. I know this because my work allows me to see the most authentic you: your soul. I am a medium and soul gardener. I came up with the term "soul gardener" because it is an umbrella for the other skills I combine: shamanism, hypnotherapy, grief counseling, remote viewing, and energy medicine. I am blessed to teach classes and speak at conferences. I train intuitives and mediums, as well as mentor people in how to create soul-centered lives.

I was one of the geeky kids who loved school and woke up every day eager to find out what gifts the day held. When I was nine, every morning and every afternoon, I would walk to the bus stop near my house. Like clockwork, my neighbor's dog Mickey would wait for me. I didn't realize it was odd that we could talk to each other. I relished our daily hug and his lick fest. One morning, I heard him say to me, "Thank you for being my friend. I will miss you." I was not sure if I had misunderstood him, but my bus soon came and I went to the back of the bus to watch Mickey as he disappeared from my view.

Mickey was hit by a car later that morning and died.

I was devastated. However, his death posed many questions for me. How did he know he was going to die? Does everyone know on some level? That experience inspired questions which have become my life's passion to explore.

As a child, I had an easy exchange with the spirit world. I knew if I prayed for someone, they could get better. I was not doing the healing, just creating a conduit for them to receive love. I have always believed in God or a power greater than my own. Although I was exposed to different religions and pathways to God, I found what works best for me is a personal path that allows me to authentically explore my soul or my connection within the universe.

My soul is the truest essence of me. It is timeless, loving, and capable of anything. When I am soul-centered, I am playful, grateful, and peaceful. I am reminded that I am part of everything and everyone around me. With that awareness, I know my actions affect everyone, as I am part of everything. I know that I am here to learn and grow. I do not seek perfection, but I yearn to be the best version of me by being 100 percent responsible for everything I do, say, think, and intend.

I have always been intuitive, able to sense and feel the people and life around me. I began to realize that this is not a unique gift, but rather a greater ability available to everyone. By seeing everything as connected, I began to understand how the language of the soul is love, because it is with deep compassion and empathy that we create peace, harmony, and unity.

As I grew up, my awareness of the soul diminished as I became distracted by the circumstances of my life. Although I was rather blessed on the outside, I was conflicted within. I had an overwhelming joy, yet there was a deep sadness and sensitivity that I often dismissed. The more I reached outside of myself for acceptance, the more my soul-centered awareness and spiritual nature faded. Other people's actions deeply impacted my confidence and security, or their words crashed in and I felt a part of me retreat.

Therapy was helpful. It taught me that what I was feeling and experiencing was necessary. However, there was still something missing. The more I told the stories about my past unfinished business, the more frequently the same types of problems appeared. My life became repetitive and I was flummoxed. I needed to have a key to me.

FEELING MY SOUL

Although I had worked as an intuitive for years, I had never considered how I was able to sense information that was known only to other people's souls. It was as if I would momentarily become them and know what their life felt like. I would feel their disappointments and longings, as well as how their individual soul graced the world. To satiate my curiosity, I began studying energy medicine. It demanded a new kind of focused attention, a deep listening. At first, I felt very little, but as my mind relaxed and I tuned in to what I was feeling without expectation, an entire universe opened for me. As I progressed in my studies, I found it magical just how many rhythms existed within the body. I could certainly sense a pulse or the blood flow, but what I started perceiving was beyond the literal structure or fluid movements within the body. I discovered that within our physical self there are diverse rhythms that function like an orchestra playing the song of our health and vitality. The more I listened, the more was revealed. My energy studies helped me to understand the connection between my intuition and the curative nature of our soul. I noticed how our beliefs, choices, families, and lifestyles create an atmosphere that surrounds our souls, which deeply affects the way our lives unfold.

I began to hear and feel things about people while I was listening to their personal energy rhythms. Sometimes wisdom would whisper near my ear or I would see snippets of their memories in my mind. Although the client would experience a renewed sense of

3

well-being and inner peace, the greater takeaway for me was that I was not doing the healing. I simply was creating a sacred space for their soul to facilitate its own healing.

Through my Western and Eastern energy medicine studies I began to recognize that our body is a beautifully functioning super machine whose majesty reflects how we live and what we do. The energy practices stressed that a whole or integrated self was a balance of our body, emotions, mind, and spiritual well-being demanding our consistent tending.

MY SOUL CALL

As my energy sensitivities increased, so did my access to the souls in the spirit world. I became hungry to learn anything and everything I could about spirit communication. I read voraciously and traveled all over the US, as well as to England, to study with known and respected mediums. The Arthur Findlay College in England, a Disneyland for mediums, was a glorious place of adventure for me. At this college preserved for the investigation and experimentation of communicating with the spirit world, I could practice my passion, explore spirit communications, and witness other mediums work, channel, and share their insights.

MIRACLES AND GRIEF

It was around this time that my father died. During his dying process, there were miraculous moments in which I received many outstanding signs, synchronicities, and insights. It was if his last gift to me was new visions into the invisible realm he was transitioning into. I sat with him while he had profound chats with his own deceased parents, visits by spirit pets we had owned, and watched as he daily recognized the angels standing at his bedside. On days of complete silence, he would suddenly awaken and continue the very conversation I was having within my own mind, as if he and I were speaking out loud. That change was pivotal to me, because it was confirmation that we were shifting our relationship from a physical one to a spiritual, soul-to-soul communication.

WALKING THE INVISIBLE PATH

In the weeks following my dad's death, I found myself in a hypnosis class. I remember thinking the first day, "I have no idea what I am doing here." However, once we learned past-life regression, I began to discover that hypnosis was an invisible path to the soul.

As my curiosity to understand the afterlife deepened, I began to draw clients to me whose deceased loved ones discussed deathbed visions and after-death experiences, as well as clients whose main interest was their soul development. It was as if the spirit world was creating a virtual classroom to satiate my deepest curiosities.

I became obsessed with my work and prayed to the spirit world to show me how to dive in more deeply.

Surrendering to the wisdom I heard within, I decided to study modern shamanism. Although I was naïve to the depth of the subject, I dove in deeply and embarked on a multiple year adventure learning the ways, history, and soul practices of shamans. I studied how many indigenous cultures approached the chakras and the human energy field that surrounds our body. I learned how to recognize both dark and light energy. I collaborated with spirit animals to discover uncharted territories within my soul that united me with an inner strength I did not know I possessed. I worked with ceremony and experienced the serenity and power of community. I journeyed into the history of my soul and its connection to the circumstances and people within my life. Shamanism was the first practice that really allowed me to transform my sadness, because I gained transformative tools that taught me how to shift the energy of my soul. Since part of the practice was working with the earth as a tool, my empathy for all living creatures, four-legged, two-legged, feathered, finned, and furred rekindled. By reconnecting to nature, I reclaimed an abundant awareness of the maternal, loving energy that I had longed for all my life. I felt as if I was looking at my life with new eyes. I could see color and beauty in everything. Most of all, my heart was filled again with hope and gratitude, just like I had when I was a child.

THE WISDOM OF THE SPIRIT WORLD

I cherish the soul conversations I have with souls in my mediumship practice. I am overwhelmed by the love and support we all have accessible to us from these invisible friends, as they share the depth of their love, passions, regrets, and hopes with those who remember them. These sessions inspire not only my clients but have changed how I live and who I am. I have been inspired to live with full responsibility for all of my thoughts, words, and actions, as well as to embrace every moment I experience with equal enthusiasm, no matter what the presentation.

MY SOUL WISH FOR YOU

My wish is to build bridges to the invisible world of your soul, so you can create a personal spirituality—one that can be easily interwoven into the fabric of your life. This book is a combination of my studies and trainings combined with my personal progression and experience working intimately with the spirit world. You'll learn how to access the wisdom of spirit through instruction, stories, and exercises you can try at home. A number of the exercises are available as audio downloads at the website for this book: http://www.newharbinger.com/41849.

To begin our journey, we will explore the landscape of your soul inside and around you by developing an ability to deeply listen and feel how your energy shifts and changes.

There is a natural evolution to the book. Our journey is meant to be fun, insightful, and personal. You can go through this book by yourself or with a group to accompany you along the path. Insights often come when others witness your progress and resistance.

You will need a few things for our journey:

1. An open heart.

2. A promise to treat yourself with kindness and patience.

3. A journal to capture your thoughts and impressions.

4. Freedom to get lost, not know, and just play like a child.

BE WILLING TO BE FOOLISH

Lastly, the tarot celebrates the Fool card as the highest or greatest teaching card, as it represents the advent of our soul's adventure in physical form. The Fool is poised on a precipice. A satchel on a stick, packed with just the essentials, rests hobo style upon his shoulder. The Fool is the "0" card to signify the infinite potential of our soul. With a white rose in hand, one foot rests upon the land and the other extends beyond the daunting cliff, hovering over a gorge below. With our next step, we will either fall or fly, yet the fool is innocent and engaged in this moment of life, gazing upward, taking in the light of the sun. He is present, thankful, and ready.

Perhaps the Fool is regarded in such high esteem because our soul knows the simple act of being fully present. This card can signify a dynamic new path, direction, or the beginning of our next life chapter with its pitfalls, ecstasies, complications, and celebrations. We are beginning such a journey now. Take a deep breath. Let's dive into the unknown and journey together upon the invisible path of your soul.

7

PART ONE

YOU ARE ETERNAL

CHAPTER 1

The Call of the Soul

Today is Gregory's birthday; he would be 36. I saw him this afternoon (not a spirit manifestation, just regular "seeing") and he was wearing a silly hat shaped like a cake with candles on it. I thought you'd get a kick out of that! He also said that I shouldn't feel sad or nostalgic or anything because it was his birthday—"I've had lots and lots of different birthdays, Ma, and now I'm not there anymore for any of them. Are you going to feel bad every day because it might be one of my birthdays?" Smart boy.

This concept has come up a great deal lately: how there is not a distant heaven but a present heaven. We seem to come in knowing, forget, and then remember, if we are lucky enough.

—Gregory's mom,
honoring her son in spirit

She came to me as a last resort. She had exhausted therapy and simply wanted to join her deceased son. It is unnatural for a child to die. She did not believe in spirit communication, as it contradicted her beliefs. Yet, something compelled her to transcend what she knew and search for a different understanding. A PhD in English, her mind had compartmentalized the happenings of her world until

September 26th, when everything she held as true imploded. During the years we knew each other, she went from a skeptic to being able to communicate with her own son. She worked harder than any client I have ever spent time with. Her fearlessness, defiance, and undying love touches my soul to this day. She may have come to me for guidance, but she changed me and I will always be grateful.

It takes courage to look at our own light and darkness with equal enthusiasm. Most of us avoid the more unconscious or dark aspects of ourselves. Perhaps this is why we can feel so very lost when our lives present adversity. Yet within these moments of seeming darkness the indelible light of our soul awaits. It is through our discovery and reawakening that true transformations begin.

Perhaps it is the loss of a loved one, fear of reaching a certain age, or surviving a pivotal or altering life experience; these episodes raise questions that cannot be answered or solved by our mind alone. We may ponder: *Why am I here? What is the meaning of life? What is my own purpose? Why do people die?* Perhaps we will first seek outside ourselves for someone or something to quench our confusion or satiate our yearnings for meaning, understanding, and purpose. However, the answers to the deeper quandaries of the human experience are not found outside of us. Instead, these dark nights of our soul are dormant spiritual opportunities to truly discover the meaning of our lives. When we stop grasping for external truth and begin surrendering into the darkness of what we do not know with openness, curiosity, and detachment, we accept the invitation to embark upon the invisible path of the soul.

FINITE AND INFINITE PATHS OF THE SOUL

You are first and foremost a spiritual being. Before you stepped into this life and long after you die, you were, always have been, and will continue to be a soul. You are nothing short of a miracle distilled into a body. You experience this life to progress your soul and the souls around you. How you live, what you do, and what you create contributes to the greater good of your soul, as well as the entire universe. That is just how important you are.

To better understand your soul, let's look at two ways of thinking about you and your life. Part of you sees yourself as a physical being, defined by your body and personality, which I will call the *finite self*. The finite self perceives life through the five physical senses. It accepts the physical world and everything around us as the only reality. Our finite self believes that everything is temporary, because all things, people, and objects within the material world die or can be destroyed. Therefore, the finite self thinks death is the end of life.

The *infinite self* or your soul knows that we are immortal and only the body dies, because the essence of us is energy or spirit. The infinite self uses two sets of senses: the five physical senses as well as the soul senses that perceive energy and the greater universe. The soul views this life as part of an endless journey and the body as a vehicle through which the infinite self experiences the material world. Let's witness the differences between viewing this world from the eyes of the finite self and the infinite self.

Finite Belief 1: I Am Mortal

The first belief of the finite self is that death is an end. No one escapes this reality. By witnessing life solely from the five physical senses, the finite self will perceive this to be true because plants, animals, people, structures, objects, and anything that is within the material world will cease to be. This perception that we die is unfathomable. It is hard to conceive of becoming nothing because we are surrounded by so much life. By seeing death as an end, the finite self will understandably be fearful of anything to do with our own mortality.

When we experience a personal loss of a loved one or witness death in the world, our five physical senses perceive we have permanently lost that person. This can make us feel brokenhearted, confused, angry, cynical, fearful, overwhelmed, and frozen—to name a few. Because our finite self relies solely upon our emotions and mind to make sense of our lives, our grief will leave us feeling helpless and lost.

Our mind will often be distracted by deep emotions and questions that the finite self alone is incapable of addressing. Death is beyond our mortal understanding. When we simply view death from the eyes of the finite self, we will always be afraid of our loved ones dying, and equally phobic about the idea of our own death.

Infinite Truth 1: I Am Immortal

The infinite self recognizes we are spiritual beings first because our soul knows we are immortal. The soul distills into a body to experience physical life. Upon death, the soul releases from its physical vessel. In this nonphysical state, souls witness their death, visit their own funerals and life celebrations, and spend time around loved ones. They seem keenly aware of being connected to this world while they begin transitioning to a nonphysical reality. When we think of our deceased loved ones, our thoughts are received like a text message, so they are still very much connected to our soul. They witness our grief, yet equally experience their own. Their soul goes through a kind of reentry adjusting to their new reality. The main difference is our infinite self does not fear death, as it is not an ending, but rather a continuation of our evolution. The infinite self knows that death is simply something that happens to the physical body when the soul has completed the lessons it came here to understand.

Finite Belief 2: Life Happens to Me

The finite self reacts to life through three channels: the ego, the emotions, and the physical senses. The ego reflects our self-worth and is often who people know us to be. Embracing and learning from our ego is an important part of the human experience. However, when the finite self does not understand an event in our life, it will

13

default first to the ego. This is problematic because the ego is only aware of one side of the story: yours. The ego will always defend the finite self, so our emotional response will be defensive. When we feel attacked, we respond as if life is happening to us. When our emotions are motivated by fear, we will feel out of control.

When our emotions are fear based, our physical senses respond by putting the body on high alert. This was all well and good when we were chased by predators, but the fight-or-flight response fear inspires has very serious long-term effects upon our mind, body, and soul. Here are a few things that happen when our body is triggered to protect itself: our blood vessels constrict, our heart rate increases, we create energy so our muscles will be ready to react, our pupils dilate, and we get tunnel vision. We are exposed every day to devastating information through our increased awareness of the events of the world. Fear is part of our daily existence. Our bodies are in fight-or-flight mode all too frequently. The long-term effects of fight-or-flight upon the body are significant, and include impaired cognitive performance, hyperglycemia, decreased bone density, high blood pressure, lowered immunity, and increased abdominal fat.

As humans continue to act disrespectfully to each other and to Mother Earth, we are creating tremendous fear. When the finite self has only the ego, emotions, and physical senses to discern the safety of the outside world, fear will dominate and we will feel helpless. We will live in a constant state of stress and worry. By believing life is happening to us, we become victim to the circumstances of our life because we perceive that we have no control. We have a hard time finding balance and peace, because we assume those values are found outside of ourselves. Therefore, we believe we will only know peace when what is outside of us is peaceful.

Infinite Truth 2: Life Happens for Me

The infinite self is introspective. It knows that we are here as spiritual beings in physical form to experience the events of our life for personal and universal evolvement. Therefore, what transpires within our lives are not random events that have no rhyme or reason—they are a magical series of spiritual opportunities, or *spiritunities*, meant to progress our soul and the world.

From this perspective, life presents us with an unlimited amount of freedom, because we are not victim to the circumstances of our lives. While we may or may not be able to change what happens, we can always control how we respond. By embracing that life is happening *for* us, we align with the soul and our spiritual nature. The reactions of our ego, emotions, and physical senses are tempered because we can look more introspectively at the gifts and blessings of these events. With this creative and spiritual response, we are participating in our becoming, and it empowers us.

The infinite self disentangles the ego, emotions, and physical senses from the circumstances of our lives. The soul nurtures and realigns our mind with the higher intelligence of the universe. We are not the only thinker, as we have unlimited access to a power greater than our own. By spiritualizing our thinking, the infinite self reminds us we are perfectly prepared for this life.

15

Looking through the eyes of the infinite self, we see our own lives and the world differently. It becomes clear that what transpires within our world is a reflection of the progress of humankind. If our life lacks harmony, we realize we must look within for understanding. There is always something we can do, at any moment. Our experiences become classrooms wherein we can grow, learn, and become the best version of ourselves. This all comes from resting in the comfort that life is happening *for* us.

Finite Belief 3: I Am My Personality

The ego of our finite self is not inherently self-reflective so to determine our self worth, it will often seek the opinion and approval of others. Many of the individuals we attract may not be in complete harmony with themselves and not great mirrors to approve and love us. They will judge and criticize us to the degree they judge and criticize themselves. Depending on the source and how much we value their opinion, they can become the critical voice within. When we seek approval from others, we will always feel insecure.

Emotionally, we can become rather dismantled and disempowered by resting our self-worth on how other people feel about us. Without a stable personal value, our relationships will feel precarious and repetitious. The finite self will not know why we are attracting the same types of people over and over again, which can make us feel isolated, ashamed, embarrassed, and unworthy. By relying more on others, we will never experience prolonged self-love, because we are not cultivating a relationship with our self.

Infinite Truth 3: I Am My Soul

You are not a separate personality and body, as your physical senses will have you believe. You are a spark of the divine intelligence and vital to the whole universe.

You are part of a source far more powerful than your own personality. As a spiritual being, you are loved and supported beyond what your finite self can comprehend. When you align with your soul, your self-worth is no longer defined by outside influences because you learn to trust your infinite self to guide you.

When you know how loved and supported you are, you can look within your life and begin to understand the *whys* of you. You become aware of yourself as a constantly evolving being who is meant to grow with the people you are surrounded by instead of being defined by them. You are meant to be exactly who and what you are right now, because your evolution serves your progress, as well as the journeys of the other souls within your life. When you know you are part of a powerful source energy, you will begin to see others as equally divine. They are merely working through their life lessons, trying to learn and grow. By loving what we do not understand within us rather than fearing it, we align more profoundly with our soul and the souls around us.

The universe needs each of us to live fully and step into each moment of our life with integrity, grace, and accountability. We are not meant to be perfect. We are meant to fumble and stumble because when we experience adversity, we evolve and learn.

Finite Belief 4: I Am an Individual

Our physical senses see everything in the world as unique but also as individual and separate. Take a moment to look at the space around you: everything has distinct forms, so nothing appears through our physical senses to be connected. Because we accept that our body and personality define our identity, we feel separate from other people. This singular perspective drives our survival, as we are wired to look into the material world to find where we fit in and where we do not. The finite self seeks communities that mirror itself and tends to dismiss or disconnect from others we do not understand or who do not mirror our beliefs. This can lead to segregation and judgment because as long as we are focused only upon our individual wants and needs, we will dismiss what is different.

As an individual, we will equally try to stand out from others. This concept breeds competition and is mirrored within our society, because we give power to those who lead or win. We are taught from an early age to admire those who are the best or have the most, so we become materialistic and get lost in the endless cycle of wanting more, never having enough, and comparing ourselves to others. We further separate ourselves by what we have, so those who have less are not equal, but those who have more are inspiring. We become obsessed with defining ourselves by what is outside or surrounds us. By seeking external power through possessions, wealth, and authority over others, we feel successful and are praised by others. Our sense of self and worth becomes defined by what we have, not by who we are. When the finite self seeks only personal gain, we become myopic and evolve very little because our possessions are more important than our soul.

Infinite Truth 4: I Am Part of the Universe

The infinite self knows we are not separate, that we are deeply connected to each other and everything, because we are all energy at our essence. This creates an automatic community with our brothers and sisters, as well as everything within the natural world. The infinite self teaches us that everything we do impacts what is within and around us in small and large ways.

This demands a very different level of engagement and responsibility in our actions, deeds, thoughts, and words. If we are part of everything, then anything that happens outside of us is connected to us as well. We are the beauty of nature, as much as we are the violence in the world. Viewing the human experience from the infinite self, we realize our reality influences the world as much as what happens in the world affects us. This is the essence of the term "as above, so below." There is reciprocity for all actions, so by holding ourselves to high standards of behavior and integrity, we positively contribute to a harmonic and respectful world.

One of the blessings within our relationships is that we witness immediately how our choices affect others. The infinite self is aware that our relationships are opportunities for our spiritual development. By "relationships," I am also including the relationship we have with nature. When we fight or resist an opportunity to evolve, or act unconsciously without considering the greater impact, that disharmony is not only reflected in the microcosm of our experience, but equally in the macrocosm of the world.

The *spiritunity*, or spiritual opportunity, is to allow the soul to guide us in all that we do, because the infinite self can be our moral compass to help us *feel* what is right and what is wrong.

The infinite self is reflective and wishes to gain wisdom from our experience. Therefore, our relationships are opportunities to see our beliefs, thoughts, words, and deeds in action. We can look fearlessly at the patterns and stumbling blocks within our lives as perfect moments given to us to deepen our connection to our soul, as well as to expand our compassion toward ourselves and others. When we are centered within our integrity and accountability, we are truly reflecting our highest good and contributing to the greatest potentials for the world.

To shift from the finite self to the infinite self requires mindfulness and a conscious shift in awareness, which is a journey we will be taking together through the rest of this book. It demands a new patience with our self as our lives transform. The gifts of living spiritually are enormous and truly transformative. To know that the events within our life unfold in perfect order may seem a bit of a leap of faith, but there is scientific substance to this truth.

UNIVERSAL LAWS

Much like we have laws within our world made by humankind to create order, the universe equally has its own laws that govern humankind as well as nature. There are two kinds of natural laws: physical and spiritual. The physical natural laws of acceleration, conservation of energy, and gravitation explain how energy behaves in the physical world. The universal laws govern the action and conduct of humankind as energetic beings. These laws directly apply to our soul, so a comfortable understanding of some of these principles helps support the knowledge that there is order in chaos or that our lives are happening for us, because we are cocreators of our experience. These laws define our actions, deeds, and thoughts as expressions of energy and apply to all aspects of creation. There are no exceptions.

Most of us are familiar with the law of attraction or the belief that what we think or believe shapes our reality. That law states that the energies of our thoughts, beliefs, actions, and words have the power to draw to us what we focus upon. What we transmit, we receive in kind. This is less about thinking positive and negative thoughts, and more an illustration of how the vibration of our soul's intentions can shape what we experience. These laws equally reflect moral fairness and mutual respect to ourselves as well as others. Although there are many spiritual laws, here are those that directly support the benefits of aligning with your infinite self.

19

The Law of Love

The greatest and most profound vibration of our soul is love. This is not romantic love; it is the expression of unconditional love. It is recognizing the divine in ourselves and one another. The sense of oneness that is created by connecting to others with unconditional love transcends our physical form. We become spirit in action. As souls, we yearn to establish this connection, because we know love as the only truth and the solution to everything. We must learn to love our neighbors, but equally fall in love with ourselves. When we practice unconditional love, we transcend the judgment, resentment, jealousy, and revenge of the mind within the finite self. Centered within the infinite self, we can aspire to love unconditionally.

The Law of Right Action

The three natural laws that work together to support right action are the law of cause and effect, the law of compensation, and the law of retribution. The law of cause and effect states that every one of our actions has an equal or balanced reaction. The laws of compensation and retribution support that depending on the intent of our original action, we will either be compensated for good works and efforts or receive retribution for any injury we have caused others.

These principles are comforting, because they imply a kind of order to our lives. We reap what we sow. It may not return to us right away, but it will in time. They create a moral compass for the soul, as well as an incentive to act with respect to others and ourselves. These laws are essentially the golden rule in action: do unto others as you would have them do unto you. From our soul's view, we are comfortable being responsible for our actions, because we understand these three laws are just and necessary for creating harmony and peace.

This equally applies to the eternity of our soul. Because we are more than just this mortal life and have existed on this earth before and may again, it is possible within this life to work through karma or the effects of past deeds. By accepting that our actions, thoughts, deeds, and words create our experience, it becomes natural to be mindful in all we do.

The Law of Harmony

Energy expresses itself in vibrations. All that we think, feel, say, or do are vibrations that we create and send out into the greater universe. This law is not the law of attraction, which is about manifesting based on what each of us creates. The law of harmony establishes a relationship between the microcosm of our life and the macrocosm of the universe. What we put out into the universe co-creates what we experience personally, but equally contributes to what transpires within the universe. This law connects us to all that happens. Therefore, the adversity and disharmony each of us creates individually becomes reflected as the state of the world. Attaining harmony comes from creating personal balance. Therefore, the macrocosm of the world will not know harmony until the microcosm of our own soul knows inner peace.

21

The Law of Polarity

Within our universe, everything has an equal opposite. The difference between the two extremes is called "polarity." A physical example is our earth. We have two poles representing the opposite extremes of our earth: the North and South Poles. This applies to hot and cold, as well as dark and light. Opposites are equally necessary, yet unique. Their opposite natures help teach us through their contrast. We would not know the power of love unless we understood the equal force of hate. The first lesson of this law is not judging or being biased to either pole. The spiritunity within this law is to transcend the judgments of the finite self that create separation and shift to the wisdom of the infinite self which honors and respects both aspects as complementary opposites that reflect wholeness.

THE SOUL BALANCE

In Chinese philosophy the principal of yin and yang embraces light and dark as complimentary and necessary partners. The yin, or the dark space, represents female energy, while the yang, or white area, is the male force. Both powers coexist within everything in the material world, including us. We are all both male and female within. The female energy of yin is receptive, soft, introspective, passive, and cool in temperature. The male yang energy is forceful, hard, expanding, active, and warm. Within each swirl of color is a dot or "eye" of the opposite energy, because there is always dark in the light and light in the dark. Neither can exist alone. Without the sky, we would not be able to witness the majesty of the stars. The deeper inference is that we are not just yin or yang, or female or male, but we are a unique combination of the energy of both values. Eastern philosophies and their alternative medicinal practices empower the individual to recognize and maintain a balance of this duality within, as it creates inner harmony and peace, as well as sustains physical and spiritual wellness.

Within our Western culture, we have a less harmonious view of light and dark. In fact, we do not recognize the balance between these two because our society sees them as opposing forces. Therefore, we emphasize their distinctions and contrasting values. Most people think of light as good and dark as bad or evil. Seeing the world this way may serve us when we attend a movie or watch a play, so we know who to root for and who to boo. But it is problematic when we overlay these characterizations on ourselves and others, because it only creates separation and judgment—neither of which reflects a spiritual or harmonious approach.

Both the black and white shapes within the circle are perfectly symmetrical and balanced. These polar opposites are in harmony. If we were to animate both the light and dark sections and remove them from the circle that holds them, each would probably swim away from the other. What maintains their relationship is the container of the circle. Think of your soul as the circle or space that holds the polarity of your finite and infinite selves together. Our soul is both light and dark, masculine and feminine. By allowing the soul to surround our experience, we can embrace our life as a series of moments that offer spectacular opportunities to grow, learn, and be the change that evolves the consciousness of the universe.

DIVINE SPARK EXERCISES

As you begin your journey into your soul, you may find that you experience moments worthy of documenting, so I suggest keeping a journal. I am a big fan of handwriting. It carries with it the energy of our soul. Here are some questions to reflect on in your journal as you consider the ideas in this chapter. Take your time with each question.

- What did you realize about your finite self?

- What did you learn about your infinite self?

- Which of the finite illusions needs your attention?

- What infinite truth do you most embody?

- What universal law do you most need to incorporate?

- Which universal law does the world need most?

When so much of our world feels beyond our control, you may wonder what you could possibly do to make things better. The good news is you. You have all the potential to deeply contribute to how we evolve. To embark upon the invisible path of the soul we must have the audacity to know our individual soul is powerful and potent. Walking this path begins with a decision to start, and that moment is now.

CHAPTER 2

Your Soul's Purpose

Every star was once darker than the night, before it awoke.

—Dejan Stojanovic,
The Sign and Its Children

My first encounter with my soul happened when I was five years old. It was 3 a.m., and I was wide awake. Although the house was still, my mind was not. My modeling debut in the Junior League fashion show was hours away, and I was busy creating all sorts of disaster scenarios, all ending with me tripping or falling on the runway. I was sincerely scared. I closed my eyes and prayed from the bottom of my soul for help.

Within moments, the walls of my bedroom began to morph and from them emerged cloudy shapes that became translucent people. These beings filled my room and surrounded my bed. Although they were unknown to me, I was not afraid at all. One loving woman came to my bedside. She looked into my eyes. Her maternal and peaceful presence immediately bathed me in comfort. As she spoke to me, her lips did not move, yet I could hear her voice speaking within my heart, as well as outside of me. She was speaking intuitively, soul to soul. "We are here to help you," she said.

In a moment, my room became two realities. When I looked to my right, the runway I was to be standing on later that day materialized. Although I was conscious of sitting upright in my bed with this lady, I was equally aware of standing on the stairs awaiting my turn to go down the runway, a future moment that had not yet happened. I was in the future and the present at the same time, yet fully conscious of each.

The runway me was fidgeting with my dress, scooping up excess tulle so that I could see my shoes and the runway stairs. I could feel my worries about tripping creating a familiar tightness in my stomach. I felt like I was truly there. My heart began to race. When my runway turn arrived, I witnessed myself climbing the stairs and walking out onto the runway without a hitch. I was so elated and relieved that I had transcended my fears, I began enthusiastically pitching the fabric rose petals from my flower girl basket into the crowd. The force of my new confidence and the ferocity with which I was throwing the petals made the audience laugh. Much like the translucent woman's compassion created an invisible bridge connecting our hearts, the laughter of the audience equally linked me to them. The petals glided from my hand into the crowd as if suspended in air. Time slowed to allow me to watch and feel everything in detail. In a moment, I became the audience. I was now seeing myself through their eyes. I could feel their compassion, support, and love. Their emotions filled the entire room, and in that moment, we were all one. Feeling that profound support and connection, I knew I could not fail.

25

With that realization, I was suddenly conscious of sitting upright in my bed. The runway and my future self dissipated and I was once again fully aware of staring into the eyes of the luminescent woman. Once she knew I was okay, she slowly began disappearing. I tried to watch her leave, but soon was fast asleep.

My life has been deeply influenced by that experience. The souls who divinely guided me that night were available to me because I asked for help. They came without personal agenda, as their individual souls were collectively focused upon nurturing me through a moment of doubt. Their loving presence made me feel supported and significant to all of them. We communicated soul to soul, a thought exchange that was heart-centered and immediate. With their guidance, I was able to witness an alternate reality and the potential of a very different outcome than the one I was creating in my mind. The fear I was projecting was truly diminishing the abundant potential of my experience. By knowing I could equally succeed, I knew I had a choice. Finally, I realized that each of our souls are surrounded by a depth of love in all the moments of our lives. If only we could live knowing that truth, how different our world could be.

The spirit world is an accessible, constant companion deeply invested in your soul's evolution.

I aspire to gift my clients with the same love and individual support that I felt that night. When I connect with my infinite self, I can see others through the eyes of my soul. Within that loving space, I fall in love with each person I work with because I am able to witness the uniqueness of their soul.

I was blessed to have that experience so early in my life. However, most of us will forget our soul. We are human beings to experience the finite self and the illusion that we are disconnected from each other. The return to the awareness of the infinite self marks the birth of our alignment with our soul and the universe.

ASPECTS OF AWARENESS

To understand the finite and infinite selves more profoundly, it's helpful to identify how the brain, mind, soul, and spirit complement and contrast with each other.

What Is the Brain?

The brain is the most complex physical organ within the body. It is in some ways like a computer, a tremendous machine capable of running the systems of our body in the background. It regulates and maintains our bones, muscles, blood flow, nerves, immunity, reproduction, excretion, digestion, and endocrine system. The brain allows us to move, sense, feel, breathe, respond, think, speak, and calculate.

The brain is equally significant to our sensory perceptions. Our physical senses translate the experiences of our lives into electrical impulses, which the receptors of the nervous system send to the brain, capturing the moments of our lives.

When a soul in the spirit world wishes to communicate with me, their soul blends with mine. Mediumship is conversation between their soul and mine. They impress their memories upon my brain and nervous system, so I will feel, see, hear, smell, and taste the moments of their lives and then share those impressions with my client. When we die, we cannot take our physical objects and possessions with us, but the sensory impressions received and stored throughout our lives as memories by our brains are ours to keep. Although our brain dies along with the physical body, it is fundamental to our soul in how it helps us process and record our lives, let alone run the magnificent landscape of our body.

What Is the Mind?

Our mind is a canvas upon which we create, imagine, analyze, process, remember, and translate our ideas. Our mind intakes the events of our life and creates our own understanding or story.

Our sensory perceptions colorize each moment based on how we interpret what is happening. When our minds are at their best, those memories are fully experienced and then stored. We can always access them in the future if they prove helpful to inform our experience. By having a neutral or objective mind, which is not influenced by prior moments, our story can be written in the moment of our lives, not dictated by unfinished business in our past.

In our childhood, our mind begins to filter our experience by how we are treated by others. What we are told, how we are raised, where we live, and what happens around us sets the tone for the first chapters of our early life. Our initial story is often coauthored, if not almost ghostwritten, by others and their ideas of us instead of our own. When we experience extraordinary moments of trauma, abandonment, health issues, or any impactful event that our mind cannot comprehend, we are unable to process and store those moments.

Because our mind is not self-reflective and lacks a spiritual awareness, we will rewind and rerun those memories. I call this "looping."
The mind alone is unable to answer *why* things happen to us, so we
will often attract similar relationships or experiences into our life
until the lesson or gift is understood. Without the spiritual wisdom
of the soul, our life will feel very repetitious.

If the mind and emotions of the finite self cannot find closure,
we will resort to judging, blaming, competing, and eventually separating from the very lessons we need to learn. Our society has
become especially good at judging others, evidence that our physical
mind is very strong and desperately in need of soulful intervention.
The goal is for our soul and mind or finite and infinite selves to
coauthor our lives.

What Is Spirit?

Spirit is the life force that is within us and surrounds everything
seen and unseen. It is the breath or spark of light that begins everything created. Spirit is synonymous with God, the Divine, Immortal
Presence, Source, or the Universe. In popular culture, it is "the
Force" mentioned in the Star Wars movies, perhaps derived from
the Hebrew word *ru'ach*, meaning spirit or life force which binds
everything together. It is a collective, limitless expanse of creative
energy or intelligence from which all that is manifest originates. We
began as spirit and return to that same source upon the death of our
physical body. Spirit is eternal, so as spiritual beings, we are also
immortal.

When the souls came into my room that night, they were individual spirits who shared a group intention to help me. Their power
was magnified because they were a unified spiritual presence.
Whereas we strive to stand out as personalities with our ego seeking
individual attention, as spiritual beings we blend and work together
with shared intentions. Spiritual beings can work in groups, collec-
tives, or as guides, but the difference is their intention is healing and
assisting. They support for our gain, not theirs. By exploring the
expanse of the universe, we gain access to all that has ever been, is,

and will be. Meditation is one such bridge that allows our infinite self to once again blend into the pure essence of all of us. Spirit and the spirit world are not destinations, but rather states of consciousness or energy, which surrounds us in all we do. It is true that heaven is within and around us always.

There are many religions in the world. Religions are belief systems that humans have created to understand the mystery of how we connect to Spirit. That source refuels and rejuvenates our infinite self, because spirit is the powerful, unconditionally loving presence of the divine. We may not find comfort with each other's religions, yet we are all tethered to the divine and its infinite wisdom of spirit.

What Is the Soul?

To experience life within the world, we must separate our spirit from the oneness of the universe. To do this, we need a container. Just like our body is the structure that keeps our organs, muscles, and bones contained, our soul is the energetic home that our spiritual essence occupies when we are connected to our physical body or seek an individual understanding of reality. Our spirit distills into our soul and animates our physical body so we can experience human life. Our soul is the bridge which connects us to the visible and invisible worlds.

When we die, our soul detaches from the physical body which can no longer sustain the eternal energy of our spirit. At this point, our individual soul will experience a kind of reentry into the spirit world to review the life we have lived and the choices we have made.

Choosing to Be Here

When the spirit world first reached out to me, and my own family and friends began connecting with me after they died, I had to look at eternity and my soul more deeply. The main question I had was: If I am immortal, then what the heck am I doing here? If my spirit knew unconditional love, why would I choose to separate myself from that loving presence and experience such incredible contrast and adversity?

What I discovered began a lifelong pursuit to understand my soul's journey. The wonderful thing about aligning with your infinite self is that once you entertain the idea that you are a spiritual being first, the universe will conspire to help you learn about your soul. I was led to people, places, and opportunities to answer all my questions. So let's begin with the big question.

Why Are You Here?

Your soul has chosen to be here in this lifetime at this moment, this place, and this time to learn, expand, and evolve. The choices you make, the people that surround you, and what you experience shape the life you live. The good news is this: we are guided, helped, and loved through every moment of our earthly experience, because there are invisible hands assisting us. Simply put, you incarnate to progress your soul. You are truly the hope of the spirit world, because as you evolve, so does the universe. That is just how important you are.

Your soul comes into this world to accomplish two different things: personal evolution and contribution to the greater good. To assist you in achieving those goals, your soul has spiritual themes woven into the potential timeline of your life. Themes are categories your soul can evolve from personally, as well as globally. Some of the themes we choose to experience include personal responsibility, communication, survival, power, gain and loss, temperance, tolerance, and spirituality.

All of our souls share one theme in particular: relationships. As spiritual beings, we understand unconditional love, community, and unity because the universe is harmonious. As humans, we must explore individual identity, which is why we have personalities and egos which create disharmony. Our relationships are meant to be explorations of love, not only toward ourselves but toward others. No matter how much we can learn independently, it is our relationships that most expand and evolve our soul. How our finite self communicates, connects, and navigates our emotions with others has evolved very little over time. Therefore, our relationships serve as the most transformative and illuminating mirrors we have to reflect how we are spiritual progressing.

YOUR SOUL FAMILY

Much like you have a family in the material world, you also have a soul family. A soul family is a group of spirits who are unconditionally invested in your soul's progress. Some remain in the spirit world and guide you, while others also incarnate to play parts within your life.

Your soul family knows all too well that what lies ahead will require a brave and courageous leap of faith. You move from the invisible world of spiritual unity, oneness, and unconditional love to the visual or material world of contrast, personality, and conditional love. Souls have often remarked in my sessions that death is the easy part; it is birth that is more difficult, because the soul leaves behind the awareness of the unlimited expanse of the universe and steps into the tiny space of a baby body. No wonder we start this experience crying.

As we prepare for our journey in physical form, there is much excitement in the spirit world, for our lives can positively inspire the future potential of this planet. So often in my sessions little spirit children run around the room announcing their impending arrival. They are interesting souls to have conversations with because they already know all about their family and are quite proud and excited to share details. They talk about the almost celebrity status of being chosen to come here, as well as share their love and enthusiasm about becoming a part of this world.

Just as our DNA carries the sum total of the genetic patterns that have repeated within our family's physical health history, our soul brings with it a kind of spiritual DNA that reflects the lessons and evolutionary progress of your family. Your individual soul has specific talents, abilities, strengths, and weaknesses intentionally set to reflect not only what you need to learn, but to also complement and contrast the personalities of those you will encounter in your life.

31

Help from Your Soul Family

Your soul family is not necessarily part of your physical or birth family, but a collection of souls who choose to work together to support, love, challenge, and align each other with their highest destiny. They remind you who you really are and what you came here to accomplish. Some members of your soul family will choose to work together lifetime after lifetime. When you meet a member of your soul family in the physical world, you may feel an immediate kinship or recognition, because your soul remembers them. They can be in your life for a long period of time or a small window, yet their influence is indelible.

Ever notice that the same cast of characters follows you from one group to another? No matter what you leave or where you move, there is always a difficult authority figure, narcissist, or pot stirrer in the group? This is a great example of how your soul family can operate. The roles that people play within your life assist your soul's evolution because they help you see what you need to evolve just as you help them grow as well. The power is noticing your patterns with people and when you are looping. We will examine our soul in relationships much more profoundly in chapter 9.

Choosing Your Parents

Within your personal family, you choose your birth parents because their strengths and weaknesses help influence and mold how you develop and grow. People who are adopted chose one set of parents to come into the world with and then another set or more to be raised by. The children not only learn from their chosen parents, but also reflect the family's evolutionary progress since children often imitate the environment around them. The impact of the role our parents play in our evolution never ceases to amaze me. So many people choose their professions because of what transpires in childhood. My sessions often focus upon healing the parent-child bond.

Collective Evolution: Soul Groups

Beyond your personal and soul families are more seasonal acquaintances called soul groups. Soul groups are a collection of souls who experience a similar event, lesson, or theme. You may encounter soul groups throughout your life within your business, schools, places of work, and spiritual or social circles. On a grander scale, soul groups can also be connected to events that effect change in the world. Soul groups can stimulate new awareness, expose truths and illusions, contribute to the rise and fall of power, demand social reform and justice, or inspire change.

Our soul can also participate in a soul group upon our death by contributing to the greater good beyond our individual life. Souls that exit in mass or tragic events are often part of a soul group.

When the Sandy Hook tragedy occurred, I was stunned. I needed to have a deeper understanding of how to spiritually frame such an event.

I went into a meditation and asked for insight. I was guided to an open field surrounded by a circle of bushes. As I looked into the shrubbery, little lights flickered. The bushes began to giggle and I became aware that each light was connected to the soul of a child. We were playing a huge game of hide and seek and I was it.

Upon that realization, the souls all floated toward me. I felt as if I was surrounded by hundreds of strands of Christmas lights. Some faces I could make out, while others just offered support and equal enthusiasm. One bright spirit light, with the most spectacular orange-red hair and perfect freckles dancing on her cheeks, came forward as their spokesperson. When I asked where I was, she said, "We are the children of the future. The earth will be ours one day. We do not understand hurting another. Sometimes we will live so when we die, you remember to listen to your heart again. Your souls forget you are living in heaven already." I was stunned by her truth. Her light glistened with the light of all who surrounded her. I thanked them all for their wisdom and soon I drifted away from their lights and opened my eyes in my office.

33

The Blessings of Challenging People

Sometimes the most frustrating and difficult people within our lives are some of our most beloved friends in the spirit world; otherwise we would never work through the more frustrating moments with them. They incarnate to help us learn, just like we equally are offering potential expansion for them. This might explain why sometimes you are quite drawn to a particular individual, and even though the relationship is maddening, you cannot seem to end it, because you are still gaining lessons from their soul. You will continue to attract similar patterns within relationships until you understand what these individuals are teaching you about yourself. The spiritunity in challenging relationships is to ask yourself what that person is triggering or revealing in you that needs your attention, love, and eventual evolution.

Perhaps this is why we become "blinded" with love, so we do not see the potential minefield we are about to enter. Yet, those experiences prove pivotal to our soul growth.

The benefit of seeing your life from the soul's point of view is that you can always look for the invisible gifts within any situation. This certainly did not happen overnight, but once I could own the fact that my soul chose the experiences of my life, I realized the benefit of being responsible for everything. That meant I could no longer blame anyone. I became more conscious that my soul would draw me to situations and individuals who were guiding me. It is a very different way of thinking, but the empowerment of that shift is life changing. I was also able to reach a point when I could forgive others and myself for past actions. Although adversity challenges us, with the eyes of the soul, we can embrace and honor such contrast as a great educator and illuminator.

Your Soul's Potential

Both your soul family and group seek to transform what is unconscious or "in the dark" into the light of consciousness. When this is accomplished, new lines of probability are created not only for your individual soul but for your soul family and the world. If we do not embrace these evolutionary opportunities, the patterns within our life simply repeat.

The reason the spirit world is so excited about your individual soul is that all it takes is for one soul in a family to positively effect change. Once a new approach or pattern is established, the destiny of all of your family—past, present, and future—can move to the next level of evolution and expand into new possible futures. Your destiny can change depending on the choices you make and the lessons you learn.

How Time Affects Your Destiny

The finite self can believe in fate or the idea that the events of our lives are predetermined. Accepting fate as truth, the finite self will equally believe that we have no control or participation in how the events of our life unfold.

Our soul perceives time as expansive, creative, and filled with infinite possibilities. Since everything is energy and it is always in a constant state of motion and evolution, time is also energy and therefore is not fixed or predetermined. Because time is energy, a waveform, it is always in a state of undefined possibility until it becomes an event. Since nothing in the future has happened yet, it is unlimited, pure potential. The infinite self knows we have free will and we are able to choose how we react within our lives. Those choices determine not only how we evolve, but different choices create new lines of potential destiny that our soul can expand into.

The Past and the Power of Learning

To understand the power of how our history affects us in this moment, think of a past event from your life. Create a time line from the moment that event happened into the future. That line represents who you were then and who you will become as a result of that experience. If you do not learn from or remain unchanged by what has happened in the past, and you continue to hold a limiting belief of that event in any particular way, your destiny line and future will either stay the same or hardly change. As long as we define our self by the events of our past, we limit what will happen to us in the future. When your past no longer limits or fearfully influences your present, you can truly live within the moment of your life.

Empowering Your Most-Desired Future

When people come to me and ask questions about their future, I would be limiting their potential if I told them what to do. I would only be reading a single line of their destiny. I aspire to help you envision the best potential future and suggest multiple scenarios, or lines of destiny, so that you can empower your present and exercise your free will to create your most desired future. Intuitives are most helpful when we envision the possibilities of your life, rather than telling you what is going to transpire and therefore dictating your future.

When beings in the spirit world mention something in your future that has yet to manifest, they are equally not deciding your future, but rather affirming the path into which you are expanding. The spirit world will never tell you what to do because your life is yours to create through your free will. The advice that is shared from the spirit world within my sessions always empowers, does not interfere with your own decisions, and never inspires fear. Many people request to know what a certain loved one in spirit wants them to do or thinks about what is currently happening. However, our spiritual loved ones know better. They will only share what will help you going forward but never impose their will over yours by telling you what to do or think. They have already had their opportunity to live—now it is your turn.

The Blessing of Forgetting

Even when we incarnate and begin this physical life with our strong intentions and great support systems, we still can forget our spiritual origins. Why does that happen? We understandably get distracted by the attributes of a physical life and the material world, and suffer a kind of spiritual amnesia.

When the finite self dominates our experience, the infinite self recedes. Our soul is always available, but being aware of the finite self only, we will be intoxicated by this world and focus mainly upon what we can gain and own. We will seek perfection, knowledge, domination, and materialistic wealth. We can be happy, but it is transitory, because what we gain in the material world we will eventually lose. I believe it is understandable and perfect that many of us forget our infinite self. That is why the dark nights of our soul are so magical and transformative; they are invitations to remember we do not walk this life alone. What we are seeking is our connection to the universe, and only our soul carries that wisdom.

Reawakening to your soul is such a great journey. To remember the eternal truth of you and realign with your infinite self blesses your life, those around you, and the whole world. Remembering renews your awareness and heightens your respect and reverence for the beauty of all that surrounds you. When you honor your sacred connection to the universe, the entire world becomes magical. This is the relationship many indigenous cultures have, and continue to nurture, within the natural world. We are truly surrounded by and infused with love and support in every moment of our lives, but to embrace this truth, we begin with understanding and honoring the sacred space of our soul.

CHAPTER 3

The Sacred Space of Your Soul

It is only with the heart that one can see rightly;
what is essential is invisible to the eye.

—Antoine de Saint-Exupery

In the 19th century, Sir Frederick William Herschel performed an experiment to measure the temperature of light. He took a prism and placed it in a ray of sun, which produced a rainbow or the spectrum of light we can see, called "visible light." He placed one thermometer in the color he was testing and two others on either side of the color band. After measuring all the spectrum's colors, he determined that the violet end of the spectrum was the coolest, while the red side emitted the most heat. When the sun shifted and the thermometers were just beyond the red spectrum of light in an apparent darkness, to his surprise, the temperature of the space beyond the visible red light was hotter than his reading of the color red. This was the first time we became aware of the light we cannot see. The invisible light beyond the red spectrum of visible light was soon named "infrared." Some snakes have specialized organs within their brains that sense thermal radiation, or infrared images, so they can see at night. Firemen use infrared cameras to look within dense smoke to detect people or animals trapped by fires.

The electromagnetic spectrum defines all the visible and invisible light we can measure. It ranges from the longer wavelengths of light which have more heat, like red, to the shorter or cooler wavelengths of violet. The invisible light beyond violet is ultraviolet, X-rays, and gamma rays. Beyond red is the invisible light of infrared, microwaves, and radio waves. In our world, accessing the Internet is done through invisible radio waves. There is so much light we cannot see, yet we trust and rely profoundly on its invisible presence.

For a moment, think of all the devices you rely upon that are wireless. What if every time you made a phone call or send a text message, a hard line or cable would connect both parties? What a tangled web of activity that would create! That visual can help you begin to understand just how many things we rely upon that are invisible.

THE INVISIBLE LANDSCAPE OF YOUR SOUL

As a baby grows inside a mother's womb within an amniotic sac, that fluid home provides the baby with protection as well as space to move and grow. The light of our soul radiates into an equally nurturing space called the aura. The human aura or your soul space is an invisible energy body of light or energetic hologram of your soul superimposed upon and radiating out from your physical body. Within this sacred space, your soul invisibly communicates data between your body and mind, as well as into the physical world and universe. Such communications reflect your essence, your purpose, intentions, beliefs, gifts, and sacred homework. Your aura is like a mini universe of your soul with all the constellations of who you have been, as well as the potentials of who you are and will be. Since you are constantly learning, the energy within your soul space equally shifts and changes. Your soul space has different layers or bands that reflect the energetic health of your body, mind, emotions, and soul. Illness and disharmony manifests first within the aura before becoming apparent within your physical body.

Let's begin sensing into this invisible landscape of your soul that surrounds your body. You can find audio for the following practice at http://www.newharbinger.com/41849.

❋ EXERCISE ❋
Sensing the Energy of Your Soul

Rub your palms together for ten seconds, like you do when you are warming your hands. When you have finished, simply hold your hands out with your palms facing each other about three or four inches apart. Focus your attention on the feeling between your palms. Slowly bring your palms within an inch of each other and then pull them very slowly apart. Repeat this a few times, slowly drawing your hands closer and then apart.

What did you notice? You may feel like there is a slight resistance between your palms, almost as if you are pulling something apart or pushing something together. You may also feel tingling. What you are feeling is the energy of your soul. Let's explore a little more.

Rub your hands together again feeling the energy between your palms. Put your hands out with your palms facing each other and hold one hand still and move the other hand slowly in a small circle around the other palm. Center your awareness on the feeling between your hands and breathe. Feel the sensations of that subtle movement in the center of the static hand. You may feel heat, tingles, or the circular motion your other hand is making. Switch directions and feel the sensations reverse. The static palm will feel the energy movements of the other hand.

This is a great exercise to do to increase your ability to feel energy. The aura surrounds everything, so gaining an awareness of your own soul space will help you become more sensitive.

You can also work with a partner. Ask them to rub their hands together, while you do the same. Have your partner put out one hand, palm facing up, then ask them to close their eyes. Put your hand about three or four inches above their open palm. Move your hand either clockwise or counterclockwise above their palm. See if they can perceive which direction your hand is moving. Once you have tried this a few times, switch and let your partner put their palm over yours so you can sense the feeling of their soul.

How did you do? The more you practice these energy exercises, the more aware you will become. It is called subtle energy for a reason, because few actual devices detect its presence. Therefore, practicing this kind of awareness is a kind of meditation, as your mind is solely focused upon one activity. Please do not get frustrated; you might be new to this. Try to keep a childlike curiosity and let it be fun. There is much more to this world than we see. To enhance your ability to perceive the invisible, let's talk about the soul senses.

41

THE SENSES OF YOUR SOUL

Our physical senses help our brain interpret our experiences in the world. Our soul equally has senses that perceive the invisible world. We have all had instincts, intuitions, hunches, bad feelings, or good vibes about people and moments within our lives. Your soul senses are multidimensional receptors that perceive other souls, nature, and the universe. Your soul senses mirror your physical senses, because your soul feels, hears, sees, smells, and tastes energy.

All of the words for the soul senses start with *clair* which comes from the French word meaning "clear." Let's look more closely at each so you can begin to understand how you already use the senses of the soul.

Clairsentience: Soul Feeling

Do you like or dislike someone almost immediately without knowing them? Can you feel comfortable or uncomfortable in a place you have never been? Do you follow your gut instincts? If so, you may rely upon your clairsentience. Your soul will feel into the energy of people, animals, places, or situations around you to sense their emotional state, health, or just see if your souls are compatible. You are feeling their soul. Clairsentients will use the word "feel" to describe their hunches—"I have a bad feeling about this"—because their instincts are part of their decision-making process. You may get goose bumps, chills, or feel cool breezes if you are able to perceive the spirit world around you. These nervous system impressions can also happen when you are receiving an affirmation from the spirit world for following your hunches. If your soul feeling is strong, you can also feel claustrophobic in large groups. Many have very sensitive stomachs. Most nurturers are born soul feelers, which is why they are so good at taking care of others, because they can sense others' needs often before the other person asks for help.

Soul feeling was the first way the spirit world worked with me. Years ago, I had a fairly significant knee surgery repairing a cracked meniscus, torn ACL, and sprained MCL. I elected to have ligament donation rather than use my own tissue. After that surgery, my gifted ACL would tingle anytime I made a contact with a soul in the spirit world.

Clairaudience: Soul Hearing

If your clairaudience is strong, you will easily hear guidance from invisible helpers or ancestors in the spirit world. Many clairaudients have one ear that is more sensitive than the other. You may hear a word or a suggestion, as if someone has whispered into your physical ear. I hear souls just outside my physical right ear, as well as inside my mind. Sometimes this experience tickles and other times, I have to ask the spirit world to turn down the volume, because these voices can be really loud. Some people with heightened soul hearing will have a hard time being in large crowds or concerts because of a sensitivity to sound. Soul hearing is very powerful, especially when you learn to trust your soul and receive spiritual guidance.

Some examples of sounds my soul hearing perceives are the timbre of souls' voices, favorite songs or music, nicknames, nature sounds, their laughs, or sounds that defined their work or hobbies. Most of all, their voices share love, healing, and their joy at having an opportunity to once again speak to you.

Clairvoyance: Soul Seeing

There are two kinds of soul sight: subjective and objective. Most mediums see spirit subjectively, through their mind's eye, as if seeing an image of a person or object like you would in a daydream. Objective soul sight is when someone truly sees a soul as if they are 100% physical. That soul will appear completely formed and present. Objective sight can be overwhelming for some because it is so intensely vivid. Most people desire the ability to see with the soul, but I have found the spirit world sometimes reserves this sense, so the other soul senses can be developed first.

Soul sight often will capture portions of a full picture, as a way for the spirit world to help you hyper focus upon a detail rather than the full image. The more you practice seeing as many details as possible, the more enhanced this skill becomes.

Here is a fun exercise to enhance your ability to see with your soul. Audio for this practice is available at http://www.newharbinger .com/41849.

✺ EXERCISE ✺
Observing a Candle

This exercise is best done in a dark room or at night. You will need a white tea light with a visible wick. Place the tea light in front of you near eye level. Make sure there is no competing background, so your eyes can simply focus upon the tea light.

Begin by lighting the tea light. Soften your gaze by relaxing your eyes, as if you're slightly sleepy. Look into the center of the candle's light.

As your focus settles, your peripheral vision will begin to observe the area beyond the outline of the flame. Keeping your gaze relaxed, and simply observe. Breathe. Give yourself a few minutes to truly witness the energy around the light. You may see different colors, as well as bands or contiguous rings. Energy is always in motion, so notice not only the movement of the flame, but of the space around it as well.

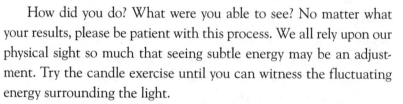

How did you do? What were you able to see? No matter what your results, please be patient with this process. We all rely upon our physical sight so much that seeing subtle energy may be an adjustment. Try the candle exercise until you can witness the fluctuating energy surrounding the light.

Surrounding every living thing are fields of radiating energy that reflects its uniqueness. You can witness auras when you are outside in nature, because everything within the natural world has such an energy field cocooning it. I find working with nature to be the easiest, as the energy of living plants is so strong and vibrant.

You can lie back and stare at a tree, softly focusing your eyes upon one of its still branches surrounded by sky. It is important that the sky or background be one solid color. Relax your gaze and look at the branch's center. With your peripheral vision, notice the branch's outline and its aura just beyond. It might look white or clear against the blue sky. The more you practice witnessing auras, the more you will become aware of their subtle energy movements. Similarly, you can hold your hand up against the sky or a dark background and witness its aura.

If you want to practice seeing the aura, have a friend stand up against a blank solid colored wall. Focus your relaxed attention upon their solar plexus. Use your expanded vision to witness the energy around their body. Now you are seeing the invisible: their soul.

Claircognizance: Soul Knowing

There are times your soul simply knows the answer to something. Soul knowing is a lightning-fast awareness of truth. This happens a great deal to me with my husband. He will misplace his coffee cup or his glasses and I will suddenly blurt out "In the garage." He doesn't give me the same funny look anymore, as he has realized there are benefits to having a medium in the house.

The last three soul senses of smell, touch, and taste are often subtler than the first senses mentioned. They work in concert with soul feeling, hearing, seeing, and knowing in mediumship sittings because they further expand the evidence or help you deepen the experience they are sharing. If I am connecting with a father in spirit, my soul feeling may sense his personality first before my soul will smell or taste his cigar.

Clairalience: The Soul's Sense of Smell

Perhaps a loved one wore a specific perfume or grew award-winning roses. When that soul wishes to let you know they are with you, you may smell roses in a place that has no flowers. Soul smells are always interesting and unexpected, because there is such a wide variety of things that have distinct odors. The spirit world uses my soul sense of smell to convey anything from coffee, gasoline, and favorite foods to heavy cologne and cleaning products. The animals in spirit give me lots of smells, because it is a strong sense of theirs. One dog cleverly gave me the smell of peanut butter and showed me the joy he had licking it off a large spoon. He went on and on about how lucky he felt to get such a big serving every night. The timing was perfect, as his owner then expressed how awful she felt about the loads of medication she had to give her dog prior to his passing, which she had mashed up and put in his evening snack. The dog was helping her reframe her guilt by thanking her for his treat.

Clairtangency: The Soul's Sense of Touch

When you physically touch an object and perceive its energy you are practicing psychometry. Some people can sense the history of an object, including its past owners, and souls who connected to the object. Psychometry is validation that our soul can leave a kind of energetic imprint. Beyond psychometry, souls equally convey memories through my sense of touch. One male soul made me feel his facial stubble as if my fingers grazed his cheek. When I shared this with his wife, she told me that she demanded he always shave before he would kiss her. It was a very simple, but intimate sharing that made his wife blush.

Clairgustance: The Soul's Sense of Taste

Food seems to be a favorite preoccupation with the spirit world. When a soul leaves their body, the need for such sustenance is no longer needed, so if souls miss anything, it is food. Souls will mention favorite recipes that have been passed down for generations or served at holidays as well as food they loved, hated, or were allergic to. Soul tasting can also include abstract things like metal, blood, and dust. One time I was two days away from the end of a rather strict cleanse. I was so tired of vegetables and water. My afternoon client's spiritual husband almost drove me to eat, because he was a known pastry chef who was meticulous about how he made his desserts. By the end of the session, I was so frustrated and starving. When I shared this with my client, she said her husband loved to tease people, especially when they were on diets. When your soul has the experience of tasting, not only is it fun, there are no calories!

The following exercise will get you in touch with your soul senses. Audio for this practice is available at http://www.newharbin ger.com/41849.

❃ EXERCISE ❃
Strengthening Your Sensory Awareness

We are going to use our soul senses throughout the book. One way to strengthen your soul senses is to work with your physical senses and your memories.

Recall a great vacation you have taken. Choose a memory where the location was very different from where you live now. Pick one snapshot of your trip, where the location is captured strongly. Imagine that you step into the photograph and sink into the fullness of the memory. Once you settle upon the visual, let your senses remind you of the deeper details you may have forgotten. Work with one sense at a time. What do you see? Really take in the entire landscape. Notice the colors, textures, and shapes of everything around you. Take your time. What do you feel? Can you feel the atmosphere of the place? Is it warm, hot, cool, or cold? Can you feel how this place makes your soul feel? Who are you connected with? What emotions come up for you? What sounds can you hear? What natural sounds are present? What man-made sounds do you hear? What sounds are close? Which ones are distant? What tastes are inspired from this place? What can you touch? What do you know being there? Write down what you remember. Do any emotions come up with any of your sense observations? Allow each sense to indulge you.

When you finish, identify your strongest sense. Now go back into the memory focusing only upon that sense and see if you can expand upon what you recall. What can you discover as if for the first time using that sense? Take as long as you wish for this exercise.

47

Our sense memory is much stronger than we realize. The souls in spirit use that very exercise when they work with me to help me feel or sense their experiences. When you have a memory, in that moment, your physical senses are working to capture your experience. When you recall a memory, you are reactivating your senses. However, our soul senses can expand such memories. Let's say your memory took place at an ocean. You can use your soul senses to further explore that location by sensing into the energy of the surrounding nature, people, or circumstances.

This is particularly powerful when the place no longer exists, as the energetic imprint of that location will always exist in time. There was a resort my family traveled to in Hawaii most of my youth, which was like a second home to me. In 2011, a tsunami hit the Kona coast and that place was destroyed. I often miss that resort, but I know it in my soul. I will revisit it and walk the grounds. As I do, I will not only remember, but my soul senses will enhance my experience, as if I am virtually experiencing it all over again. Since it was a significant place to me, my emotions will equally rise. I will feel the way the wind blew and see details in the lava. Since 2011, a number of the souls connected to that place have died. When I journey with my soul senses, I will often see souls from the spirit world equally walking around remembering. Although I cannot return physically, I can certainly revisit with my soul.

The best way to strengthen your soul senses is to capture the memories of your own life through your physical senses. It is a great mindfulness exercise to find a place and surrender to your senses. Take in the environment one sense at a time. You will be amazed how deeply you can connect. Memories of our life and the feelings we have are what we do take from this world. Expanding your sense awareness in your daily life not only enhances your soul senses; it deepens your connection to your life.

DEEPENING YOUR CONNECTION WITH YOUR OWN SOUL

The soul senses are great bridges to witness and perceive not only the environment, people, and events of your life, but the spirit world around you. Sometimes when you begin something new, your mind can interrupt the fun. The finite self loves to interrupt and judge when you are trying something new. To empower that process, let's focus not upon *what* the mind is saying, but rather upon the *feeling* of your thoughts. By focusing upon the energy, not the thought, we are shifting our awareness from the mind to the soul. You can find audio for the following awareness-building practice at http://www .newharbinger.com/41849.

✸ EXERCISE ✸
Shifting from your Mind to Your Soul

This is a great exercise to try anytime your thinking gets loud. Bring to mind a situation that is currently unsettled in your life. Once the situation is strong in your mind, locate the place in your body where you think about this situation. Where is your mental energy the strongest? Once you identify that location, just observe. How does the energy move? Is it quick, slow, pointy, swirling? Try to define the movement of the energy of this thinking place. After you have a strong connection to it, ask yourself:

"Where do I feel the energy of this situation within my body?"

Take a moment and feel with your soul. Feel within your body. Where do you *feel* this situation? Start at your toes and scan your entire body all the way up to the top of your head, noticing each place that feels active. Take your time, because your mind will want to get the answer right away. This is a discovery of feeling, so try not to rush. You may notice a few places. Pay particular attention to your torso. Isolate the one place where you feel the energy of this situation the most strongly. Your thinking place and feeling place should be different. Focus upon the feeling location. What does the energy of that place feel like? Is it swirling, pulsing, or shaking? Is it evenly distributed or is it more on the right or left side of this area? Draw what it looks like in your mind's eye. Is it rhythmic or beating like your heart or does it feel tight and slow moving? Are there images or symbols that you can perceive as you connect to this place? Train yourself to not just notice where there is energy, but get curious about how it moves and makes you feel. Is there a temperature: hot or cold? Is there an emotion that connects to this place as well? If so, simply honor your feelings. Take your time.

Finally, place your hand on the location of your body where you feel this situation. How does it feel to put your hand there? For some it is quite nurturing, as your hand can often calm your feelings and relax the location.

Take a deep breath in and then release the exercise. Clear your awareness as if you are wiping clean a dry-erase board.

❂

For many, the thinking place is somewhere around the head. This makes logical sense, so it is important to let yourself discover the place where your mind or your finite self operates. How about the feeling place? Your feeling location tends to fall within your torso either around the heart or solar plexus. If you experienced a different location, please know it is perfect. We will call that location where you feel your thoughts "the seat of your soul."

When you begin working with your soul senses and perceiving energy, I suggest putting your hand upon your soul seat. It is a reminder to your infinite self that you are doing soul work. Knowing the central location of your soul within your body is helpful, because when you are in the middle of your day and your mind is busy, you can simply put your hand on that place, drop your attention into that space, and connect with your soul. Simply observing the energy of your mind within your body will allow your mind to relax. The seat of your soul is always a place of discovery and comfort.

RESPECTING YOUR SOUL AND THE SOULS OF OTHERS

When we connect within to our soul seat, we are aligning with our infinite self. We are honoring both selves by witnessing how we think and feel and allowing the soul to gain self-awareness. In this way, respecting our soul expands our consciousness that everything around us is sacred.

Indigenous people walked this earth spiritually connected to everything, as they recognized that a Great Spirit was the creator of all things and that all things were of spirit. Anytime an animal was killed, the hunter would acknowledge and thank the spirit of the creature for giving its life for the sustenance of the tribe. This gratitude, awareness, and connection to Mother Earth and all her creatures is not only respectful and gracious; it is soulful.

If someone's door is closed, you knock before entering. It is polite and respectful. The same concept applies when we do any kind of energy work, offer intuitive insight, or give spiritual messages. We can get very excited about what we perceive. Self-exploration is always permitted, but sharing our perceptions without the permission of another is disrespectful. We must honor that not everyone is ready, open, or wants to receive our intuitive epiphanies. Permission extends to all living things: people, as well as plants and animals. By asking permission before sharing information, we are acknowledging the free will of each soul, as well as honoring spirit.

Honoring the sacred in all you do changes your relationship with your world. Your compassion and empathy will equally expand. As you continue to hone your skills, you will be amazed at the feeling of gratitude a flower emits when you ask permission to partake in its beauty.

51

Here's a guided meditation to help you anchor into the seat of your soul. You can find audio for this practice at http://www.newhar binger.com/41849.

❋ MEDITATION ❋
Witnessing Your Soul Space

Preparing Your Physical Space

When you meditate, you need a place where you will not be disturbed, because you will be in a slightly altered brain state. It is not wise to have reality come crashing in. Turn off your tech-nology and sit or lie down where you are completely comfort-able. You can lie down, but if you tend to fall asleep like I do, you might want to sit up instead so you can be alert and relaxed and not just have a good nap. The goal is to focus your full attention on the exercise. Feel free to record it before you begin.

Take deep breaths in and exhale before beginning.

Imagine that standing on the top of your head is a "little you": perfect, playful, and ready to explore. Take in this little version of your soul. Perhaps it is you now or perhaps a version of you from childhood. Look at your hair, body, and what you are wearing on your feet. You have everything you need for this journey, including any superhero tools you may need: goggles, sabers, a head lamp, and even a jet pack.

Standing on top of your head, let "little you" look up and witness the top of your aura. That space of your soul is at least three or four feet above your head. Relax and let your soul senses begin to expand into that space above you.

Now imagine looking to the right and see your energy field extending out from your body to your side another three or four feet. Let your awareness feel into the space. Look to the left and feel into that space between you and the edge of your energy field. Your aura surrounds the entire physical body, so let your perceptions explore a few feet in front of your physical body, as well as behind you. Take your time. Feel the fullness of the space of your soul.

Your aura also penetrates the earth a few feet below you, so sense that feeling of extending into the ground below, as if you are growing roots. Use your soul feeling. How does your soul feel to connect to the earth?

Activate "little you"'s power pack and start to fly within your aura. As you explore, remember you can look forward, back, up, down, and side to side, but stay within your soul space. Take your time. Use your soul senses: How do you feel, what do you see, what do you know, what do you hear, what do you taste, what can you touch, and what do you smell? Give yourself a few minutes to really explore your personal universe. When you are finished perceiving with your soul senses, fly back to the top of your head. Take a nice deep breath in and exhale. When you are ready, open your eyes.

✷

53

How was that? You are just beginning to use your soul senses. It is perfectly normal to have some senses be easier or more accessible. What soul sense was your strongest? Which soul sense was a surprise to you? We will be practicing with these all throughout the book, so let this simply be the beginning. No mental traffic allowed.

Here is a meditation to help you begin to connect to your soul within your body. Audio for this meditation is available at http://www.newharbinger.com/41849.

✷ MEDITATION ✷
Exploring the Seat of Your Soul

Again imagine "little you" standing on the top of your head. Once you have that visual, notice that directly in front of you is an elevator. Let the doors of the elevator open. Step in and turn around to face the doors as they begin to close. Push the button that takes you to the seat of your soul.

The elevator travels down within your body, descending vertebra by vertebra. Once it stops, the elevator doors open and you step out into your soul seat. You are not within your physical body, but instead some place in nature. Open your soul senses to perceive this invisible landscape of your soul. Whatever you perceive is perfect. Just allow yourself to play within your soul like a child.

Within this place, you can move in all directions: forward, backward, side to side, up, and down. Like an owl, you can look in all directions simply by choosing to do so. Using your soul sight, what can you see? What does the landscape look like? Are there colors? Are you alone in this space or are spiritual loved ones or pets present?

Feel with your soul into this landscape. Pick a word that describes how you feel in this place.

What does your soul know in this place?

What can your soul taste, touch, or smell?

Go to the spot that feels most sacred to you. Take your time and find it. Where are you drawn to go? Imagine yourself walking or floating there. Let "little you" sit or lie down to relax and release anything that no longer serves you melt into the ground or space below you. Simply relax into this place. Visualize the air around you filling with small, moving lights. You are witnessing fireflies. Watch as they decorate the space around you like playful stars. Each begins to follow the other and line up. Watch them form words in the sky letter by letter. They are forming a word or sentence that is a gift to your soul. What is the message you receive? The iridescent letters illuminate the entire landscape. As the light strengthens so does the presence of unconditional love to fill the entire space around you. The light from your gift blends into the space, filling it with divine light. Ask to be of service to the universe and to honor and listen to your soul, and any other souls you work with, for everyone's highest good.

Remain in this space and simply relax.

When you are ready, thank your soul and all that is within this place for always radiating love and light. Find your way back to the elevator. Walk in, turn around, and let the doors close. Push the top floor button and take the ride back up to the top of your head. When the doors open, step out.

When you are ready, take a few deep breaths and then open your eyes.

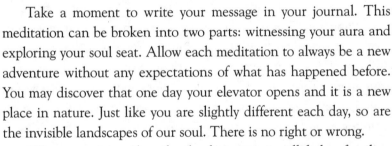

Take a moment to write your message in your journal. This meditation can be broken into two parts: witnessing your aura and exploring your soul seat. Allow each meditation to always be a new adventure without any expectations of what has happened before. You may discover that one day your elevator opens and it is a new place in nature. Just like you are slightly different each day, so are the invisible landscapes of our soul. There is no right or wrong.

When you visit a place for the first time, it will feel unfamiliar, yet over time you become more comfortable there. Your soul seat is an unknown place right now, but dropping into your soul seat on a daily basis is a great way to check in with how you are feeling, as well as get a heads-up about the day. The fireflies can give you a word for the day or you can simply visit the space to rejuvenate. You can work with each of the soul senses independently and see what you can sense. Your soul seat is a very sacred space and deserves to be honored and explored. The benefit of revisiting places within meditation is that you are creating a virtual location in time and place that your soul becomes comfortable visiting. The more you visit this center, the more real it becomes. The spirit world is eager to work with your soul, so your commitment to being open and receptive is a great start and your soul space is a perfect location to begin.

DAILY PRACTICES TO HONOR THE SACRED SPACE OF YOUR SOUL

Now that you have expanded your soul senses by exploring your soul's seat, you will relate with your own soul in new and profound ways. Much like the weather alters from day to day, so does your soul. When you check into your soul on a regular basis, you will begin to see patterns, colors, people, and guides appear. You can explore the energy of your soul space surrounding you or drop into your soul seat. Your aura can indicate upcoming events and issues, as well as indicate what is up for you. Your soul seat can help you manage your mind differently and explore the depth of your soul. I have had many clues and signs appear to me prior to pivotal events within the space of my soul. The spirit world cannot stop things from happening, but if we are paying attention, we can receive signs that can certainly help you become aware. You can receive messages and notice just how profoundly the happenings of your life affect your energy. You might record daily changes and observations within your journal. The more you check into your soul and witness its ever-changing landscape, the more confidence you will have with trusting your soul and its connection to the universe.

DIVINE SPARK EXERCISES

Before we jump into the next chapter, honor yourself with some observations about the exercises and concepts within this chapter. Here are some suggestions of questions to ask:

- What was it like sensing into your soul space?

- How did it feel to sense the energy of your soul by rubbing your hands together? If you worked with a partner, what was your shared experience?

- Which soul sense is strongest for you? Which is not so familiar? Feeling, knowing, hearing, seeing, tasting, touching, or tasting?

- Where does the energy of your mind, or finite self, nest in your body?

- Where is the seat of your soul, or infinite self?

- What did your "little you" look like? If you wish, take some crayons or pens and draw your impressions.

- What were the highlights of your meditation exploring your aura and the seat of your soul?

- What was the word or message you received from the fireflies? How does it apply to your life or taking the journey of this book?

- What did you learn about your soul?

SOUL LISTENING

Let's finish the chapter by practicing something essential: listening to your soul. Put your hand where you feel your soul seat or infinite self. Take a few deep breaths. Ask your infinite self:

"Please give me a spiritual message about my soul and what I am learning."

Release the need to know and just open your soul senses and breathe. You do not have to do anything, as the information will be given to you. Your soul senses will receive answers through images, symbols, words, and feelings. You may hear or see words or phrases, see an object or symbol, feel love around you or sense a soul in the spirit world. Simply sit and allow information to come to you. When you are given a message, write it down. Next, ask "What word best describes my soul right now?" Write down the first word or symbol you receive, even if it does not make sense. This is a great exercise to do each morning. You may find the messages you receive in the morning will become clear as the day progresses. Sometimes the words will repeat, as will the messages. Just listen and trust what you receive.

57

We have done a few exercises within this chapter. You may find some easy and others more difficult. Learning to trust the voice of your soul will enhance all of your soul senses. You can ask for help and guidance throughout the day as well. Feel free to change the questions depending on your needs. Most of all, enjoy this new exploration of trusting that your soul is always guided.

In this chapter, we have been building your connection to your soul senses. In the next chapter, we'll go even further and explore how the universe of your soul connects to your physical body through energy centers called chakras. We will explore each using the soul senses and expand your ability to witness the invisible world of your soul.

CHAPTER 4

The Infinite Light of Your Soul

Let me, O let me bathe my soul in colors;
let me swallow the sunset and drink the rainbow.

—Kahlil Gibran

In the past chapter we talked about the electromagnetic spectrum of light or all the light we can see. The chemical processes within our body, as well as the energy of our soul, emit light and color. Although most of our bioluminescence is invisible to us, color influences our mood, emotions, and mind more profoundly that we realize. The spectrum of reds, oranges, yellows, greens, blues, and violets exists not only in our surrounding environments, but equally within our soul space. Before we dive into the landscape of our soul more specifically, I want to spend time allowing you to witness your relationship to color subjectively. Please do the following exercise before continuing on with this chapter, as it creates an important framework we will use throughout the book.

❊ EXERCISE ❊
Soul Sensing Color

The objective of this exercise is to allow your soul senses to experience color without the finite self unconsciously dictating what you have been told or believe color to be. To do this, go to the *Soul Conversations* website at http://www.newharbinger.com /41849. You will be shown a number of full screen colors. Take your time with each and allow your soul senses to explore the color deeply. Have a journal so you can write down your observations. Allow your observations to be a stream of consciousness so there is no need for anything to make sense. Just trust what you perceive and receive. Use the detailed instructions below to guide you. You can download an audio version of these instructions at the website if you'd like to listen and follow along.

Exercise: Soul Sensing Color

To begin, drop your awareness into your soul seat. Take a few deep breaths in and when you are ready, begin the color slide exercise. Click to see the first color. Allow your soul senses one by one to explore the color. Begin with soul feeling: How does this color make you feel? What emotion do you associate with the color? Where do you feel that color inside your body? Soul hearing: What sounds do you hear? What does this color have to say to you? Soul knowing: What do you know about this color? Soul seeing: What images, symbols, and pictures do you see connected to this color? If this color needed help, what color would balance it? Soul smelling: What smells do you experience? Soul tasting: What do you taste holding this color? All your soul senses: What gift does this color give you? What word is associated with this color? Write down any additional observations about the color slide you are viewing before moving on to the next color. Go through each of the colors exploring each one fully. When you are finished, take a deep breath in and exhale the exercise.

Our response to color can be very strong. What color did you like the most? What color did you not enjoy? What color soothed your soul the most? Which gift was most relevant?

EXPLORING THE INFINITE WITHIN YOUR SOUL

The light of our soul contains all the colors of the rainbow. The electromagnetic fields of your soul space are comprised of two parts: the auric field and the chakras. The auric field or your soul space you experienced in the last chapter is comprised of subtle layers or fields that are maps of your physical, emotional, mental, and spiritual well-being. In order for your soul space to connect to your physical body, it uses funnels or energy vortexes called chakras.

Chakra is a Sanskrit word meaning "wheels of light." These channels allow the energy of what you experience to be processed by your soul. Although there are many chakras within our soul space recognized by different traditions, we are going to focus upon the seven main chakras recognized in Hindu beliefs.

61

The chakras receive, transmit, digest, and assimilate the vibrations of your experiences, memories, relationships, patterns, habits, dreams, and visions. By learning to work with these centers, you can positively affect your personal health, empowerment, and inner peace. Additionally, each is a mini universe that allows you to explore your soul in unique and powerful ways. Each center develops during certain ages of our lives, so what you experience and how you hold those early memories directly correlates to the level of vibrational health and well-being each chakra radiates. Each connects to different endocrine glands and organs, and communicates with the brain via the nerve branches or plexus.

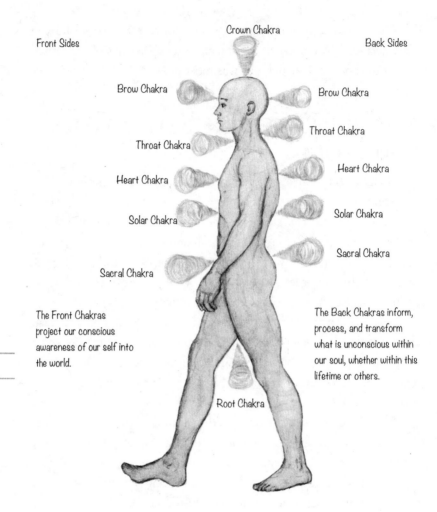

Front Sides

Crown Chakra

Back Sides

Brow Chakra

Brow Chakra

Throat Chakra

Throat Chakra

Heart Chakra

Heart Chakra

Solar Chakra

Solar Chakra

Sacral Chakra

Sacral Chakra

The Front Chakras
project our conscious
awareness of our self into
the world.

The Back Chakras inform,
process, and transform
what is unconscious within
our soul, whether within this
lifetime or others.

Root Chakra

Muladhara: Your Root Chakra

The root chakra is called Muladhara in Sanskrit meaning base
or support. Aptly named for its location at the lower sacral spine,
this chakra connects or grounds your soul into our physical body
and connects you to the earth.

The root chakra's health reflects your will to live. The safer and
more secure your soul feels, the more innocently you can live and
connect to your life and this world. The glands associated with this
chakra are the adrenals, because when your safety is at risk this

gland governs the fight-or-flight response. Since this chakra develops when you are an infant, how much you were held, comforted, and included in your environment, as well as how safe you felt as a child, will greatly affect how it develops. Whether you experience continual fear or unabiding love, this chakra will always reflect the degree to which your past informs your present.

This base chakra energizes the pelvis, legs, feet, lymphatic system, and our bones, as well as our muscles and blood. When the root chakras energies are balanced, we will have strong overall health, easily connect to people and our environment, move fluidly and with flexibility within our world, and be able to release and let go of what does not serve us. When this chakra is unbalanced, we can be lethargic, depressed, myopic in our focus, self-destructive, or disconnect easily from people, places, and our spiritual awareness.

Each chakra partners with an auric layer that radiates from your body into your soul space. The layer closest to your body connects to the first chakra. The connection between the chakras and aura is thrilling, because the information of our soul is not only within us, but radiates around us like a mini universe. Therefore, an energy practitioner can work within the subtle fields of your soul space to affect change within your body because these bands of energy transmit information. Each field emits color and surrounds our body uniquely. To me, the first auric layer appears as electric blue lines of light that sheathe your body like a net. It radiates about two inches out from your physical body.

Since the root chakra points downward toward the earth, it is recharged through our connection to our body as well as the earth. Walking, dancing, hiking, gardening, yoga, tai chi, trampolines, and running all rejuvenate the energy of the root chakra. All the days of our physical lives, we are within the energy field of the earth. Therefore, having a conscious relationship with the earth and all of nature nourishes and recharges our soul. Many indigenous cultures live with the awareness that they are guests upon the land, so opening up that root chakra and mindfully extending into the earth is a gorgeous way to begin your day. You can find audio for the rooting practice below at http://www.newharbinger.com/41849.

✹ EXERCISE ✹
Rooting into the Earth

You can do this exercise either sitting or standing barefoot upon the earth. Begin by inhaling, setting the intention to deeply connect to the earth around you. On your exhale, image roots extending from your feet into the earth below you. Take the next few breaths to simply melt into Mother Earth. Imagine your soul descending into the roots and feeling into the soil below. When you have finished, relax your breathing and open your soul senses. Can you feel the energy of the earth? What do you notice? How does it feel to be held within her? On your next inhale, imagine bringing that cool, deep, powerful energy of the earth up into your feet, legs, and into that root chakra. Drink in her love. Notice where your physical body relaxes as you connect. Sit and simply bathe yourself in the nurturing and loving energy of Mother Earth. Take a deep breath in and when you are ready, open your eyes.

As mentioned in the previous chapter, the electromagnetic spectrum of light ranges from the longer wavelengths of red to the shorter wavelengths of violet. That spectrum is overlaid upon the chakras, so the lowest spectrum color of red is associated with the base or root chakra because it equally has the lowest frequency of the seven main centers. However, I have found color within the body changes profoundly, so if you experience other colors present within your chakras than the ones assigned, please trust what you perceive. Part of the journey of the soul is to find your authentic truth, so be willing to trust what you perceive.

Take a moment to review what you observed about the color red in the first exercise. What was the color that balances red? You can also "feed" or nurture each chakra with color. Drop your focus into the root chakra and imagine "little you" has a paintbrush, spray paint, roller, or paint gun and color that chakra in the healing color that feels right to you. You can also try giving your root chakra green. Green is red's complementary color on the color wheel. Since green is the color of the heart chakra, which represents our capacity to give and receive love, gifting yourself green may comfort your feelings of lack of security, connectedness, or fear. Once you finish painting your chakra or filling it with the chosen color, release the visuals and just sit feeling into your root center. Notice the difference in how you feel simply by adding color.

Svadhisthana: Your Sacral Chakra

The second or sacral chakra is the seat of your creativity, sensuality, and relationships. Located between the hips in the lower abdomen, the associated glands are the testes and ovaries. In Sanskrit, the name Svadhisthana translates to *sva*, "self" or "one's own," and *adhisthana*, or "dwelling place." During the ages of six months to two and a half years old, this chakra develops as we create our sense of identity and begin to explore our instinctual physical and emotional desires of attraction and relationships. Not only are we learning about extending love, but we are consciously receiving and feeling love. That is why this chakra also deals with the love of the self. The orange color of the sacral chakra stimulates our desire to create, so it makes sense its energy is located within the woman in her womb. Influenced by the element of water, we give birth to our passions and gain the fearlessness to gift this world with our uniqueness. This energy center relates to our reproductive organs, large and small intestines, appendix, and bladder, as well as the sacral nerve plexus. When our second chakra is balanced, we are creative, vital, and sensual. We are gentle with ourselves and others, enjoy intimacy, and are willing to express mercy and joy. When out of balance, we are at odds with ourselves and others. We may doubt and be discouraged easily, feel rejected, abandoned, worried, or codependent. We can fear physical contact or intimacy, and experience restriction of sexual and emotional freedom. When these emotions are more prominent, our desire to create and express joy will be visibly diminished.

65

It saddens me how many of us experience some form of physical violation. For almost 15 years, I was continually drawing experiences to me that revolved around this chakra. I felt like I was in a perpetual loop. Thank goodness I learned to work with my soul for it gave me the freedom to reframe those experiences, thus releasing the fear of intimacy I held onto. Therapy, energy medicine, personal realizations, and finally shamanism helped me shift how I was allowing those past experiences to shadow my present. I did not realize the depth to which my fear was limiting my experiences both creatively and in my relationships. There is nothing the soul cannot transcend. We are incredibly flexible and always evolving so we can gain much from looking at what happens in our lives and learning from those moments.

The soul lesson of this chakra is to allow our souls to create and express freely within all we do, including our relationships, without the need to solicit empathy for the hardships we have endured.

The second layer of the auric field is called the emotional body. This layer extends out from the body, overlaying the first layer and then extending beyond it a few inches. Because it overlaps the physical layer, the emotional body affects the physical body. As each field of the aura expands, it must first blend into the previous layers. This visual can help you understand just how much our health is dependent upon overall wellness between our body, mind, emotions, and soul. Unlike the more fixed physical layer, the movement of the emotional body is very fluid, like water. This layer feels like I am swimming in my client's soul.

To nurture this chakra, create. Whether you paint, draw, act, imagine, journal, blog, write music or poetry, play a musical instrument, or craft, our passion drives the beauty of our authenticity. Orange is a combination of red and yellow, which are the colors of the root chakra below and the next chakra above. Color bathe this chakra with orange or with the color you discovered that heals orange. You can also feed the sacral chakra the cool and calming color of blue, its complementary color, especially if you are feeling highly emotional.

Manipura: Your Solar Plexus Chakra

One of the most active chakras in developing mediums and intuitives is the bright yellow glow of the third chakra, positioned between the navel and sternum. The home of soul feeling, the third chakra radiates the fiery essence of our personal power like a sun. Named Manipura or the "city of gems," it relates to the endocrine gland of the pancreas, which assists in digestion through the production of hormones and enzymes. Besides digestion, the solar plexus chakra governs the internal organs of the stomach, liver, gall bladder, spleen, kidney, and large intestine and connects to the solar nerve plexus.

This chakra develops during the ages of two and a half to four, when we begin exploring independence, decision-making, and digesting the reaction and opinions of others. When the solar plexus is balanced, we feel empowered, authentically decisive, persistent, faithful, trusting, and even-tempered. We feel we belong. Within this center we begin to mentally understand our emotions. When out of balance, we can be highly emotional and overly sensitive, self-conscious, intimidated, passive or irrational, self-destructive, overwhelmed, and distrustful. The soul lesson of the third chakra is to know you are worthy and have a right to have your own ideas and beliefs while allowing the opinions of others. If you grew up having a sensitive stomach, this chakra has great insight for you. It is the chakra of the nurturer, because it is highly utilized by people who naturally sense into their environment and connect to the feelings of others first, often before their own.

The solar plexus chakra corresponds to the mental body of the aura. Like the first layer, it appears more dense or tight in feeling. If a person is very much in their finite self, this layer will feel tight like a rubber band, almost as if it is compressing the emotional body, especially if a person is overly judgmental or critical toward themselves or others. The invitation of this chakra is to honor your feelings. If we are very reliant upon the acknowledgement or opinions of others, we may find the health of this chakra will be greatly impacted.

To honor your solar plexus, drink up the energy of the sun by spending time outside in daylight. Since this center focuses upon creating balance between your mind and your emotions, notice when you experience fear and try things that make you uncomfortable. Try adventure sports or any opportunity that requires you to investigate your fear response. I love zip lining, because I have a fear of jumping. My thoughts and body begin to tense, and yet, the feeling of jumping off something is an absolute adrenaline rush for me. It makes me realize that my finite self will set limitations that are not always true. You could try scuba diving, hiking, kayaking, cycling, rock climbing, or sky diving. The goal is to remind yourself of the strength of your soul. Your finite self may engage, but you will gain clarity by understanding the difference between a perceived limitation and the infinite power of your soul. By focusing upon discipline and pushing your ideas of what is possible, your infinite self will govern this center. To nurture your third chakra, feed it yellow, your healing color for yellow, or the complementary color of violet.

Most of our soul work or evolutionary homework connects to at least one of the first three chakras. The lower chakras invite us to dive into our history and transform how we feel and think about the experiences of our lives. It is about bringing what is unconscious into consciousness. If we simply retell what has happened to us without introspection, we will remain unchanged. The goal is to objectively witness the stories we tell over and over. The more we step into ourselves and love our evolution, the stronger and healthier these centers become.

Anahata: Your Heart Chakra

Our heart chakra is poetically centered between the three lower and upper chakras. In Sanskrit, Anahata means the "unstruck sound" which mystics observed as the melody of the universe. Corresponding to the cardiac nerve plexus, this chakra relates to the heart, lungs, diaphragm, breasts, circulatory and respiratory systems, as well as the vagus nerve that extends from the brain stem into the abdomen. There are differing opinions on the endocrine gland that relates to the heart chakra. Some believe it is the thymus or high heart, which assists our body in maintaining a strong immune system, while others suggest it is the heart itself, which is considered an endocrine gland since it produces and releases hormones. This chakra develops during the ages of four and a half to seven, as we begin to experience the impact of receiving and giving love.

When the heart chakra is healthy, we work well with others and act with an equal awareness of our mind and heart. We see the world as a benevolent place and realize we must nurture, accept, and forgive ourselves as well as others. When this chakra is out of balance, our motivation will be self-centered so we may be selfish, withdrawn, and unmotivated. We can become spiteful toward others, competitive, codependent, or jealous. The soul lesson of the heart is to focus on love as the answer to all situations. Our heart so beautifully illustrates that we are either connecting or disconnecting to life with our actions, thoughts, and deeds.

The heart chakra connects to the fourth layer of our auric field, called the astral body. Within this fluid layer, I can see the status of past and present relationships, as well as the health of each. I also find this layer begins the interchange of the spirit world, as guides, healers, and loved ones often show up within this layer. I will see spirit doctors stand within this band of the auric field and perform healing upon the mind, emotions, and physical body by channeling the unconditional love of the spirit world. When someone is truly ready to consciously shift how they feel and think about a past experience, I have seen individuals receive dynamic spiritual healing within this layer.

69

To nurture our heart chakra, take in the beauty of nature, play with a child or a pet, laugh, give without the need for recognition, and simply love. Do something for someone else: write a thank you note, call an old friend, send someone flowers, or simply drop your attention into the area of your heart and send love to another. The ultimate goal of the heart chakra is to find where you can be of service to this world, as that is the highest love we can share. To honor your heart chakra, feed it the heart chakra colors of green or pink or your healing color for green, or its complementary color of red.

The upper chakras are often referred to as the more spiritual centers within our soul space. Theoretically, as we ascend and work through the lower chakras lessons, we are transforming what has been unconsciousness into full consciousness. Through the heart we learn to love all that is. As we progress into the higher chakras, we are taking our ordinary awareness and blending it with the higher consciousness of the universe.

Vishuddha: Your Throat Chakra

Holding the idea of heaven on earth, we step into Vishuddha, the fifth chakra, located in the throat. Its name means "purification." Within this chakra, we facilitate our own healing and empowerment by allowing our voice to always be a blend of the authenticity of our soul and the wisdom of spirit. This center of communication and self-expression connects to the laryngeal nerve plexus, as well as the throat, larynx, gums, teeth, jaw, ears, mouth, and glands of the thyroid and parathyroid. This chakra develops during the ages of eight to thirteen. Mediums and intuitives who communicate with spirit though soul hearing do so through this chakra. When the rich blue of a healthy throat chakra radiates, we are able to listen, communicate, make good decisions, and stand by our ideals. We are open to spiritual guidance and allow the wisdom of the universe to blend with our thoughts and words. Conversely, when this chakra is not balanced, we have unclear communication and lack spiritual inspiration. We can be indecisive, stubborn, and listen only to our own opinion. The soul lesson of the throat chakra is to engage in empowered communication by clearly stating our needs and wants, while integrating heart-centered listening that balances our own ideas with the wisdom of the spirit world.

I have always felt any spoken words are prayers. Anything we utter verbally or think internally releases into our soul space and the world. Our intentions contribute to and shape what we experience more profoundly than we recognize. Imagine what our world would be without the words of Martin Luther King, "I have a dream," or those from Sir Winston Churchill's speech during World War II,

"We shall never surrender." Being a Gemini, I am fascinated by the power of communication. It takes tenacity and courage to speak your mind. The throat chakra has a direct correlation to the third chakra of personal empowerment. So often our ability to speak our truth depends on how worthy we feel. If we draw only on others' opinions of us and are not centered in our soul, we will doubt our ability to effectively contribute to the world. Our voice will be diminished, if not silent. By embracing the healing and transformative opportunities that await you, you will find new courage and support to confidently share your thoughts and words with the world.

The fifth layer of the auric field is the soul body. Within that layer, I witness the purpose of your soul, lessons that are influencing this incarnation, and the impact of past lives. I can also witness guides that are working specifically with your soul communication. This is especially true with writers, actors, communicators, and motivational or inspirational speakers.

You can nurture your fifth chakra by singing, learning to say no, expressing how you feel, effectively communicating, and listening to the voice of the spirit world. By owning the value of your thoughts and feelings, you will have the courage to speak your mind and share your opinions. To nurture your throat chakra, color bathe it in blue, your healing color for blue, or orange as its complementary color.

Ajna: Your Third Eye Chakra

The sixth chakra, Ajna, means "command" or "unlimited power" and is often called the third eye or brow chakra. In Vedic times, the center of the forehead was adorned with a *bindi* or red dot symbolizing the goal of attaining purity of thought. In the ancient Egyptian religions, this spot was known as *aten* which symbolized an awakened third eye that could also see the soul within. Perhaps this is why many practices use this as an internal focus point for our physical eyes to look at when we are meditating as it allows us to see what is unseen. The sixth chakra allows our mind to blend our intuition with the logic and practicality of the left brain and the right brain's creativity. This center energizes the eyes, brain, sinuses, hypothalamus, and central nervous system. This chakra develops in adolescence, which is why many children experience their intuition blooming in their teenage years. The associated gland to the brow chakra is the pituitary. The purple of this chakra radiates health when we can "see" clearly through our illusions, take responsibility for all of our actions, and remain curious, open, and hopeful. When we step into these gifts, we begin to trust that things happen for our highest good, so we can celebrate all moments of our life. We blend the wisdom and intuition of the infinite self with the mind and emotional response of the finite self. When out of balance, we will be unreasonable, ignorant, or indifferent to our spiritual nature, lack in self-knowledge, and become judgmental of others as well as ourselves. The soul lesson of the sixth chakra is to embrace the concept that we cocreate our happiness or unhappiness depending on how we perceive and envision our life.

The sixth chakra connects to the celestial layer of the aura. Within this more fluid layer, I witness a gateway to the spirit world and the guides and ancestors that support my client's soul journey. This layer often informs me about future potential destiny lines that connect to my client's inspirational ideas or passions, as well as who supports them in the spirit world.

Yoga is fantastic for all our energy centers, but in particular the sixth chakra, because you are mindfully connecting your physical, mental, and emotional centers with your spiritual awareness while practicing. Trusting and following your instincts, trusting signs you receive, and building your relationship with spirit all enhance this center. Most of all, meditation is truly the bridge that will connect you to your infinite self. To nurture your brow chakra, feed it the color violet, your healing color, or its complementary color of yellow.

Sahasrara: Your Crown Chakra

Finally, we arrive at the seventh chakra. Sahasrara is the lotus of a thousand petals. It is located at the top of the head and radiates white with gold and violet hues. It is the location of enlightenment and self-realization because it connects us to our higher guidance, the universe, and our deepest spiritual nature. When we pray sincerely or ask from our soul for help, this center, along with the energy of our heart, bridges to the divine. Sahasrara renews our entire body and supports all of our organs, glands, and cells. It connects to the pineal gland, which is the first gland to develop in a fetus and orchestrates all of the endocrine glands within our body. This chakra develops during our early adult years and throughout our life. When the crown chakra is balanced, we are grateful, count our blessings, are humble, inspire and support others, as we know everything is an extension of ourselves. When imbalanced, we can be proud, self-righteous, arrogant, overly intellectual, and dismissive of others.

The crown chakra connects to the universal layer. This layer appears much like the golden halos depicted in early religious paintings. The more spiritually developed a person has become, the more illuminated this layer appears to me. The soul lesson of the crown chakra is to continually remain open to our spiritual development and integrate that wisdom into how we live, act, and behave.

73

To understand the chakras and how they function is a deep journey of which I have just skimmed the surface. It is important to honor your energy body as much as your physical body. Every emotion, thought, and action has a vibration that moves within and around your soul space. Those vibrations equally release into the world, just as you sense the vibrations from other souls.

REJUVENATING YOUR SOUL SPACE

This mindfulness is not just about karma and personal repercussions. Much like we have environmental pollution, we either embellish or diminish the world around us based on how we act toward ourselves and others. When our finite self has thoughts and feelings that are impure, those thought vibrations not only impact the person we are not in harmony with, they will most certainly have an impact within our own soul space. This is why personal responsibility is so vital. The first step is realizing we contribute to our own happiness and our overall health by the choices we make. The second step is realizing we are also impacting what is around us.

You can download the audio for the following practice at http://www.newharbinger.com/41849.

✸ EXERCISE ✸
Waterfall Rejuvenation

Much like you choose to cleanse your physical body, your soul also gains great healing from receiving light. The following exercise will help you refresh and renew your soul space.

Bring your attention to the top of your head. Imagine you are "little you" standing on top of your head. An elevator door opens before you. You step in, turn around to face the door, and push the button to take you to the seat of your soul. The elevator descends and as the doors open, you find yourself somewhere in nature. As your soul senses expand, you hear the sound of water. Follow the sound until you find where the water is. You may find a lake, a stream, or an ocean. Go there now.

As you stand by the water, you see a waterfall in the distance. The water is inviting. It is shallow enough for you to walk in. Step into the water and go toward the waterfall. You feel the atmosphere shift around you as the water begins to alternate in color, becoming all the hues of the rainbow. You feel so comfortable and safe that you step into the waterfall. Feel each color as it clears, cleanses, and rejuvenates your soul space starting above your head and moving down into each chakra one by one, bathing it with color.

Feel the power and security of red bathing your crown, third, throat, heart, solar plexus, sacral, and root chakras, then releasing into the water, coloring it vibrant red. The waterfall shifts from red to orange. Let the orange water clear, cleanse, and rejuvenate your soul space, as it gifts your soul with creativity, passion, and sensuality. Feel the orange color enlightening your crown, third, throat, heart, solar plexus, sacral, and root chakras until all the water around you glows orange. The water-fall catches the light of sun and radiates empowered yellow to clear, cleanse, and rejuvenate your soul space. Feel it come into each chakra one by one. As it leaves the root chakra, witness the vibrant yellow flowing into the water and feel yourself sur-rounded with your pure potential and empowerment.

Sense into the area around you. Feel connected to all the life that surrounds this place. The foliage around you sends lush, verdant hues of green to the waterfall. Watch as the cool and loving green water washes into your soul space and into each chakra, filling you with unconditional love and acceptance of yourself and everyone in your life. As the green releases into the water below you, witness how it reabsorbs into nature. You are at one with all around you.

Above the waterfall appears a guide or ancestor. Watch as they shift the water to a rich deep blue. As it cascades into your soul space, feel the cool and tranquil blue water enter each chakra from your crown to your root, flushing out any miscom-munication or misunderstanding. Feel your connection to your voice and authenticity as the blue seeps into the water below. Feel your deep connection to this guide. Thank them for their presence and support. They disappear in a cloud of purple light that infuses the water and fills your soul space. It gently nour-ishes and cleanses each chakra, starting at your crown and ending with your root. Let go of any fear or doubts. Notice how your intuition and inner guidance return and are strengthened by this color as it pools into the water below you. Finally, the night sky opens above you and all the stars send light to create a single ray that pools into the waterfall, electrifying it with the crystalized light of the unconditional love of the universe. Witness how this bright white light illuminates the water and enters your soul space. It radiates into your crown, third eye, throat, heart, solar plexus, sacral, and root chakras until you are pure light. Feel the power of the light and your connection to everything within you and around you. Gently let the light recede and the colors of the environment surrounding you return. Look around you and see what is different. Thank the waterfall and this place for honoring your soul. Walk back across the water, back to the shore, and back to the elevator. As the door opens, you step in. As you turn around, the elevator doors close and take you back up to the top of your head where you step out completely refreshed and rejuvenated. Take a nice deep breath in and exhale. When you are ready, open your eyes.

You can use the above exercise to cleanse a single chakra as well. Simply go to your soul space, find the waterfall, and intend that the color most needed to heal your soul fill the water. Do not worry if you cannot see everything; just follow my words and trust the adventure. Your inner vision will increase over time. Guided meditations will help all of your soul senses develop.

You can also work with the healing properties of water when you are bathing. Imagine in the shower that the water falling down around you is rainbow colored. Simply ask that the color that best soothes your soul clear and cleanse you. When you feel that color release, then envision white light washing down upon you, rejuvenating and empowering your soul. Setting intentions is a very powerful creative force of the soul.

DIVINE SPARK EXERCISES

In this chapter, we have focused a great deal on the invisible landscape of your soul. Becoming aware of your soul space can not only tell you how you are feeling but can help you perceive when a situation within your life is having a greater impact than you might realize. To keep strengthening your abilities to perceive your luminous energy field, experiment with any of the following exercises.

- *Connecting Your Body to Your Soul:* Most illnesses and physical issues begin within our aura first as an energetic imbalance. Therefore, when you have a physical issue, look at the chakra that connects to that part of your body. Review the conditions that create imbalance in that center and see how they may apply to your life. By focusing upon the emotional or mental symptoms and which chakra they correlate to—1st—security and safety, 2nd—relationships or passion, 3rd—personal empowerment, 4th—giving or receiving love, 5th—communication and speaking your truth, 6th—trusting your intuition, or 7th—nurturing your spiritual connections—you will get a deeper insight into how your body mirrors your mind and emotions.

- *Colorizing Your Chakras:* Practice feeding your chakras with color. Have "little you" venture into each chakra and discover what it feels like to sit within each center and bathe it in color.

- *Adorning with Your Color:* If your soul craves a certain color, you can wear it. Notice how you feel walking around wearing that color. Do people treat or respond to you differently? What feels new?

77

- *Flower Power:* Fill your healing space or home with flowers of your healing color. This is especially helpful if your situation surrounds a relationship within your home. The vitality of the flowers will represent the health of your situation. By having them in the room, you will be unconsciously reminding yourself of your chakra homework.

- *Natural Color Support:* Once you identify the chakra you are focusing upon, find stones or crystals of that color. You can buy jewelry or simply put colored stones around your environment to support your focus and attention upon your energetic health and well-being.

- *Get Out the Crayons:* Get a box of crayons. When you are working with your chakras, what you may encounter often relates to a specific relationship or situation. Draw the energy of how you feel. You are not so much drawing a literal interpretation, but rather a symbolic one. You can use a different color for each soul sense. When you are finished, take a look at what you drew. If it represents something you wish to shift or release, hold the piece of paper between your hands and place it in front of your heart. Pray for guidance to understand the gift of the situation and surrender to the outcome. When you have completed that task, find a safe location like an outdoor fire pit and burn your drawing. This process helps you detach not only from the circumstance, but from the outcome. Detachment is a higher skill of the soul, as we must be willing to let go of what we wish to happen and trust that what actually transpires will be best for everyone.

Now that you have a clearer view of your personal soul space, let's take a voyage into the universe using your soul senses.

PART TWO

CONNECTING TO THE UNIVERSE

CHAPTER 5

Your Soul and the Universe

Magic happens when you tell the universe what you want it to do for you. Miracles happen when you ask how you can be of service to the universe.

—Marianne Williamson

It was our first wedding anniversary. In the morning, my husband called to share his love and in the afternoon, he called to say he had been let go from a job he had had most of his life. It was the oddest day. Instead of giving in to the fear looming around me, I decided to surrender to the invisible presence I relied upon daily. I simply said, "Let me be of service." Within a few weeks, my business booked out for a few months and I have never looked back. It was an affirmation from the spirit world that I had found my calling. It was as if everything in my life suddenly made sense. Many of the decisions I had made and the diverse jobs I had held each gifted me with a piece of my soul puzzle that now all fit together. Since my prayer was answered so profoundly, I have dedicated my life to the pursuit of spirit communication and being of service in any way I can to the spirit world.

81

I have an insatiable curiosity about mediumship. Beyond my personal studies and voracious researching, I started wondering how this soul-to-soul exchange transpired. I began observing the energy space around my clients, as well as noting shifts and changes within my own soul space when the spirit world was present.

I observed a funnel above my soul space that appeared like a floating wormhole or chakra. It seemed to facilitate the energy exchange between my soul and the universe. The whitest light of spirit filled the funnel and poured into my crown chakra. I felt mesmerized by a calming presence that distilled into and recharged my soul. It was as if I was shifting from a physical being into my spiritual essence. The more I relaxed into the experience and expanded into my soul space, the more I felt part of the universe.

That feeling of oneness is the perfect space for me to work. Within that sacred space, I am soul-centered. I begin all of my sessions that way, because in that space, I know I will listen like a child to the spirit world and truly honor my client. I do not have to worry about being "protected" because I am surrounded by the pure light of Spirit.

The following is a meditation to help you experience and practice feeling the flow of light entering and expanding into your soul space. Audio for this practice is available at http://www.newharbinger.com/41849.

✹ EXERCISE ✹
Opening to Receive

Begin by taking a two-part breath through your nose. Inhale in a quick sip of air followed by a full inhale. Hold your inhale for four seconds. Now release the breath again in two parts with a quick exhale through the nose followed by a full exhale using the muscles of your abdomen to push all the air out. Hold before you inhale. Repeat this three times, breathing in, holding for four counts, exhaling out and holding again for another few seconds. Good. Allow your breathing to find its own natural rhythm.

Imagine a large ball of white light floating above you. This circle of light expands, becoming a large disk of white, iridescent light spinning and filling the entire space above you. This light is loving, warm, and nurturing. Witness this light as it begins to gently swirl into a funnel floating down toward your head.

Allow this white light to touch into your energy field and witness it swirl down into your crown chakra. Perhaps you feel tingling or goose bumps as the energy of the universe connects with your soul space.

Feel the spinning funnel of light coming into and filling your crown chakra, cleansing and clearing anything that no longer serves you. The light descends into your third eye, filling the center of your head with brilliant white light. It cleanses and rejuvenates your vision and intuition.

The light easily drops into your throat chakra, clearing, releasing, and relaxing this communication center.

Let the light descend into your heart chakra, clearing, cleansing, and releasing anything issues around relationships and love.

As the light descends into your solar plexus, feel the light replenishing you with personal empowerment, authenticity, and confidence.

The light illuminates the sacral chakra. Allow the light to rejuvenate your creativity and cleanse your relationships.

Finally, witness the light swirling into your root chakra at the base of your spine, filling that place with security and personal balance.

Witness how this column of universal light connects all of your energy centers in a column of white iridescent light. Allow this shaft of light to continue descending your body, into your thighs, knees, ankles, and into your feet, so you are completely bathed in this light.

The light continues downward into the ground below your feet, creating a pool of light mirroring the disc above your head. Take a few moments to sense and feel this luminescent love and intelligence above as well as below you. Above and below.

The disc below your feet begins to radiate lines of light like roots that extend out from the disc below and rise up around you, as if cocooning you in a sacred ball of light. Witness these lines of light as they fill your soul space and reconnect to the disc above your head. Practice following the path of light beginning with the disc above your head, spiraling down into your chakras one by one, down your body and into the ground. Let the light pool beneath you, filling the disc below and then branching up, encasing you in a luminescent ball reconnecting above your head. Use your soul feeling to sense this current above you, flowing within you, pooling below you and then surrounding you. At this time, state this intention: "I allow guidance to honor my highest good. I am open and grateful." Take a few minutes and allow your soul to receive healing, insight, or simply bathe in the rapture of blending with the spirit world. Spend a few minutes simply observing how you feel surrounded by this presence. When you are ready to finish, begin by thanking the light for all you have received. Imagine the funnel of light connected to your crown chakra beginning to recede. Watch as it coils back into the pool of light above your head. The pool of light diminishes and slowly disappears. Take a few deep breaths in and exhale. When you are ready, open your eyes.

Take a few minutes to write down your observations. Sometimes it helps to draw a picture of how you perceive energy working within your soul space.

This meditation will help you visualize a pathway so you can practice receiving energy and be open to the guidance. It is a great exercise to do before any soul work or any of the exercises in this book, as it aligns you with your infinite self and the universe.

HOW YOUR SOUL TRANSMITS

When you allow the energy of the universe in, you are *receiving*. When you *transmit*, you are sending out your intentions, desires, and visions into the universe. Since you are asking the universe for support, the more you can empower your words and thoughts in this process, the greater results you will experience. Let's look at how your soul transmits thoughts, intentions, and desires into the universe, through prayer and intention.

Prayer

The purest transmission of love our soul performs is when we pray for others. We are reminding that soul of their eternal connection to a power greater than their own. In adversity, the finite self can lose hope and become fearful. Through prayer, we are simply sending light to their soul, reminding them of their magnificence. Prayer allows the universe to work through us and graces everyone.

When we pray for ourselves, we are asking the spirit world to assist us. Since we have free will, the spirit world cannot help unless invited. By asking for help, we are acknowledging that our soul does not operate alone.

The finite self may not understand prayer, because it does not recognize an intelligence beyond its own. The finite self will refer to past events as a mechanism to fix or solve a current problem. When those attempts fail, the finite self will sometimes feel victimized by what has transpired.

The infinite self knows the soul's journey within the physical world is unfolding as it should. It knows that we cocreate our life through our beliefs, choices, and actions, which can create expanded lines of destiny depending on our ability to engage our lessons and transform. Therefore, when we pray from our soul, we are requesting that the universe assist us in creating and manifesting our best life by invoking divine intervention.

Soul-centered prayer has three parts: asking, receiving, and thanking. When we pray, we are first asking for help and shifting to our soul. We are transcending the limited beliefs of the finite self and opening to the awareness of a power greater than our own.

The second step of prayer is receiving. To allow such support, we must feel we are worthy of this intervention. Receiving also demands surrendering and detaching to the outcome. This may seem contradictory, but it is necessary. When we pray from our soul and ask the universe for assistance, what may transpire may not be how our finite self envisions the result. Detachment allows our prayers to manifest for our highest good or the highest good of others, without our need to control the outcome.

The last step of prayer is gratitude. Our gratitude affirms our connection to spirit and places our intention fully within our heart.

Intention

To navigate within the physical world, we use a GPS that plots a route between where we are and where we wish to go. Similarly, to navigate the nonphysical world, we set an intention, desiring and envisioning a potential destiny, and use our free will to cocreate our life. Intentions are created when we have the courage to acknowledge our dreams and desires, and envision ourselves becoming them.

When you explored the energy field both within and around you at the beginning of this chapter, you were observing your soul space. It is important to know that your atmosphere is greatly affected by the quality of your thoughts. Therefore, intentions can be a great tool to fill the space of your soul with ideas and thoughts that support your desires and how you wish your life to feel. Intentions are strongest when they have an excitement attached. To understand how your mind and intentions mirror in your body, here is a simple kinesiology experiment for you to try. Audio for this exercise is available at http://www.newharbinger.com/41849.

✹ EXERCISE ✹
Muscle Testing

Muscle testing is a great way to quickly test how your body responds to a thought or an outside stimulus. To do this, begin with your right hand and touch your right middle finger to your right thumb. Push the pads of each finger together to form a circle. Using the same two fingers on the left hand, put them into the right hand's circle and try to break the right hand's circle apart. Repeat this a few times until you feel comfortable with the process. What you are doing is finding your baseline, or the normal level of strength you exert.

Part One: To test how strengthened you are by positive feelings, relax your hands and think of something that you simply adore: a pet, child, partner, food, movie, or song, something that simply fills your heart with joy. Let the memory fill you. When your recall is strong, take the middle finger and thumb of your right hand and make a circle. Focus upon pushing the pads of those fingers together. To test the force of positive thought, take two fingers of your left hand and try to break the circle made by your right hand apart. Notice how thinking about something you love affects your strength. It should be difficult for your left hand to break apart your right finger's circle.

Part Two: Now let's test your physical strength when you are focused upon a more challenging situation. Relax your hands and think of a difficult situation or one that makes you sad. Perhaps it is a missed opportunity or a recent disappointment; find something that makes you feel forlorn. When that feeling is palpable, make the circle with your right hand and try to break it open with your left hand. Keep thinking of the adversity or sadness and see how it affects your overall strength.

✹

87

What you will discover is a simple illustration of the power our thoughts and emotions have upon our body to either strengthen it or to weaken it. Even though our thoughts are invisible, they emit energy. That energy affects the landscape of our soul tremendously, so the surrounding energy then impacts our body.

We may not always be in a great mood or optimistic. We will have emotions that relate to what we experience, but what also affects the vibrancy of our soul are the residual feelings, positive or negative, that we have relating to a person, event, or situation. The initial emotion can subside, yet if we continue to feel fear, guilt, resentment, grief, judgment, hatred, anger, apathy, shame, and blame, we emit those energies into the space of our soul. Setting intentions is a powerful way to help our soul radiate higher vibratory thoughts and desires that can balance and positively shift our energy from how we have felt to how we wish to feel.

The most empowered intentions have five parts: forming, feeling, planting, thanking, and detaching. Begin by forming your intention. Ask yourself what it is you wish to manifest or create. Visioning this way, you are creating a potential destiny line for your soul, so be specific, optimistic, and clear. To energize your intention, begin with the statement, "I am": "I am listening from my heart," or "I am clearly communicating my needs." Now your intention is activated and happening.

Next imagine what it will be like when your intention manifests. To do this, close your eyes and state your intention. Imagine your hope or desire as if you are living it now. What would it be like to have that intention manifest? Can you capture the excitement with your soul senses? How do you feel? What do you see? What do you smell? What can you taste, touch, and know at that moment? Root the feeling of the intention within your soul.

Now that you formed your intention and have felt your excitement as it manifests, drop your attention into your soul seat. Observe how that natural space reflects the beauty of your desire. How does the energy of your intention equally manifest within your soul space?

Imagine your desire is a seed and plant it within your soul seat. Watch it take root. As it does, thank your intention for bringing to your soul exactly what is best for you.

At this point, you have formed your intention, felt its empowerment, planted it, and expressed gratitude for its manifestation. The last step is to detach from any expectations regarding your intention, knowing that you have created a perfect energetic pathway for the most desired result to manifest.

You can experiment for a day with setting intentions and notice what subtle changes occur. Try taking a moment before all of your activities to set an intention, or a vision, of what you wish to happen or how you wish to be within each experience. Let's say you are working on a project; you could say, "I am grateful for the clear, creative, and visionary ideas that inspire my work." If you are spending time with a loved one, you might say, "I am fully present and heart-centered in all my relationships." In this way, intentions can be a great mindfulness practice for journeying consciously toward your soul's evolution within your relationships, work, and in any goals you wish to accomplish.

89

HOW YOUR SOUL RECEIVES GUIDANCE

Prayer and intention are two ways your soul transmits your needs to the universe. However, to partake in the infinite offerings of the universe, we must practice receiving. We receive best centered within the infinite self. From that space, we can truly listen and learn.

Meditation

When I first began meditating, I loved guided meditations, because following someone's words helped me relax and begin exploring what I have come to know as the eternity of my soul. Much like a writer can look at a blank page and be overwhelmed, many have the same feeling of discouragement when it comes to their efforts to quiet their mind. The use of guided meditations can ease this distress. You will never be without thoughts, so in meditation the mind is not empty but rather deliberately focused upon one idea or what is happening in the present moment. That conscious attention allows your soul senses to fully engage and receive. Learning this process can take time, but it is within that stillness the soft, subtle voice of the universe can be heard. If sitting still and alone in meditation does not engage you at first, there are many different ways to meditate.

I love sound meditations, in which I simply witness what I can hear within my environment. This meditation you can do with your eyes open, but I find I concentrate more upon hearing with my eyes closed. When you are ready, just listen. Really hear all of the nuances of what surrounds you. Whether you are inside or outside, you will be amazed at how much sound escapes your everyday awareness. You can also listen to your body, breath, and heartbeat. Your surroundings will contain a blending of natural and man-made sounds all synthesizing into a perfect symphony.

Sometimes it is easier for people beginning the practice of meditation to work in a group. My meditation circle meets twice a month to meditate together. Whether we set specific intentions or not, I am amazed how often we share the same visions or experiences. Whether we have intended to gain greater knowledge about a world event or the universe, we have received incredible collective insight and wisdom. My ability to hear the spirit world is greatly enhanced by sitting in a spirit or meditation circle.

To sit in such a circle, it is important to gather like-minded and soul- centered individuals whose intention is to surrender to the universe and be of service to each other. Always begin with a group prayer that aligns the participants with their infinite self. You could even use the meditation I offered at the start of this chapter. Whether you practice reading each other or just sitting with the intention to blend with the spirit world, you will find these meetings graceful and powerful.

Meditation is called a practice, because it truly is. It is a lifelong journey into your soul and your connection to the universe. If you find it blissful, great. If you find it challenging, don't be discouraged. You are different each day, so some days your mind will be peaceful and other days more distracted. Just allow yourself to be exactly where you are and simply be open to the experience. With practice, you will find meditation is a stunning way to deepen your awareness of all the light we cannot see.

Intuitions and Promptings

Our soul senses are always connected to the infinite self and the universe. We receive intuitive insight when our soul senses expand into the energy around us and perceive energy information. Promptings are when the spirit world joins the conversation and helps our soul. This is why developing a healthy relationship with your soul senses is so important. Understanding these energy indicators is like having a spiritual GPS that can help you make empowered decisions throughout your life.

Years ago, I had signed up to take a class offered by English medium Robert Brown in the Bahamas. He had invited psychic medium John Edward to be his featured guest. A month after I signed up to take the workshop, I suddenly got a huge wave of emotions about the trip. Instead of sitting with my feelings and trying to understand them from my soul senses, I went with my finite self and I cancelled the trip.

However, the universe kept sending me promptings that the trip was necessary and important. I kept seeing and hearing things related to the Bahamas. Students asked me if I knew any English mediums that taught in the US. Medium John Edward was frequently brought up by numerous people asking me if I knew him. The final prompting was when my mom asked me about that trip. I realized the universe was trying to get my attention. I reinvestigated the fear I had originally sensed and realized I was feeling excitement and possibility as well as fear. Once I finished the meditation, I contacted Robert's office and he graciously allowed me back into the conference.

That trip changed my professional career. It was at that conference that I aligned with John Edward. Soon after, he asked me to host a show on InfiniteQuest, a site he cocreated with astrologer Alan Oken to support the exploration of all things metaphysical. It also created a fabulous friendship and working relationship with English medium Robert Brown. I met a great tribe of new friends and a soul sister. So much changed in my career because of that trip. Had I let the feeling of fear go uninvestigated by my soul, I would have missed out on so much.

Feelings of fear should always be investigated. They certainly deserve our respect. However, sometimes what we may feel as fear is just a power greater than our own. As in the example above, what I was feeling wasn't fear, it was the next best version of me waiting to happen.

Signs

Our loved ones in spirit miss us as much as we miss them. There are a variety of ways they communicate with us by manipulating our immediate environment, nature, or impressing upon our soul senses.

Our technology can be disturbed. Some souls in spirit send texts, call phones, or alter our technology so a photo pops up or voice mail is heard. We can also see shadows or glimpses of our loved ones. Some people may actually see their loved one once again in physical form. Photographs can demonstrate their presence with orbs, cloudy formations, or impressive impressions within the photograph resembling their physical self.

Within the natural world, animals like butterflies, hummingbirds, dragonflies, ladybugs, or other winged creatures can be symbolic signs of their presence. The metaphors of wings inspire gaining perspective, flying above our circumstances, and traveling light, as well as remind us to look up when our grief can feel debilitating. Sometimes a wild animal will cross your path and their presence is a sign. Your loved one does not become the animal, but the spirit world can manipulate time and matter to help a synchronistic event happen. What is significant is the timing of that animal's presence, sometimes combined with a strong soul feeling, that will make us think of our loved one in spirit. Sometimes rainbows, cloud formations, weather conditions, or shooting stars seem to be equally heaven sent.

Many times we receive physical signs like pennies, feathers, crystals, stones, or heart-shaped objects. We can see messages on billboards, TV advertisements, signage, license plates, or email subject lines. We can hear songs, people with similar voice tones, our loved one's name, or natural sounds they loved. Some even hear their loved one speaking. We may smell their cologne, perfume, cigar, or alcohol. Sometimes we need to be overwhelmed with repetitious signs or synchronicities in order for our soul to pay attention.

Our soul senses can experience chills, breezes, or goose bumps that are not from our environment. Temperature drops frequently happen when souls are present. You can feel their presence with your soul or feel the touch of their hand. I will get chills or goose bumps in my mediumship sittings, especially when a soul is excited about seeing someone or emphasizing a point. To experience more signs that your loved ones are present, simply give them permission to overwhelm you. Not only will you receive confirmation, but by being open for signs and symbols, you will truly be in the moment of your life.

93

Dreams

A vivid dream is when you are sleeping and you have a soul-to-soul encounter with a loved one in spirit that is so real it feels like it actually happened. A regular dream tends to have parts that defy logic, like being in a department store with a zebra. A vivid or lucid dream is a virtual visitation. Sometimes this is the first way a soul will communicate with us after they have died. When we are grieving, our soul space is filled with confusion, sadness, and feelings that make it challenging for us just to get through the day. Knowing our soul would benefit from love and support, our loved ones will reach out in dreams. We are more accessible when we are sleeping than we are within our grief, because our finite self is not trying to process the great change we are experiencing. Their souls miss us too, so the healing that transpires is mutual.

Physical Phenomena

Some souls seem to enjoy communicating with us by manipulating energy, disrupting our environment with intentional electrical phenomena. Much like our intentions send out wavelengths of our desires and dreams, souls can transmit into our environment. They send out wavelengths that create apparent disturbances which affect surrounding electricity, causing lights to flicker, television to malfunction, and voice-activated machinery to chat without provocation.

In all of my sessions, I give the spirit world permission to play within my workspace. After all, this is a continuing experiment not only with my ability to communicate, but also for their souls to connect into the physical world. During readings, I leave my computer email program open because my incoming emails create a "ping" sound. The timing of sounds from my computer often emphasizes messages I am receiving from spirit. It happens so often now that even my clients are in on the fun.

The year after my father's death was particularly difficult for me. One December night, I was working a father-daughter dance and missing him terribly. While I was out, our Christmas tree light strand started blinking like crazy. In frustration, my husband unplugged the tree completely, but it continued to blink for over three minutes.

A spirit husband promised his wife he would begin bringing her feathers because he had finally communicated to her after years of silence. At the session's end, she leaned down to gather her belongings and on top of her purse was a single white feather.

Another time, I was sitting with a lovely young woman who was clearly in an unhealthy relationship. Each time I sensed into her boyfriend's energy, I became more aware of his self-interest and potential for being unfaithful. No matter what I said or how I phrased the information, she was clearly just in love with him and it was not sinking in. I simply asked for some spiritual help to emphasize that he might not respect her enough. In that moment, I felt her father in the spirit world step forward and the room shifted slightly. The next thing I knew, the metaphysical instrumental background music I had been playing suddenly switched to a rap station with artist Taio Cruz's song "Break Your Heart." She recognized the song, looked at me wide eyed, and I simply said, "You might take that as a sign."

During a reading for a family, I connected to the soul of a young man who had passed instantly in a motorcycle accident. He was a sassy spirit, with a healthy ego, who began to saunter about the room, flexing his muscles and running his fingers through his hair. He made me smile at once. His aunt validated that he liked being the center of attention. He energetically walked over to her and stood right next to a vase I had on the table with two single flowers in it. I had just said, "He liked walking a fine line, and loved pushing life to its limits" when all of a sudden the two flowers in the vase switched positions. I had never seen anything like it before and all five of us witnessed the movement! The flowers went home with his aunt, along with a very strong indication he was up to his usual mischievous behavior.

95

TOOLS FOR HEARING THE VOICE OF THE UNIVERSE

During the next few chapters, we will be deeply exploring soul-to-soul and spirit communication. However, before we begin, I want to go over some tools and techniques you can use to open your soul senses to your soul's wisdom as well as the intelligence of the universe. Tools are physical objects that help build your vocabulary and trust with the spirit world. Much like some people benefit greatly from following guided meditations to relax into exploring their soul senses, tools can help you see into the energy of your soul.

Tarot Cards

My trust in the spirit world developed and deepened with my exploration of the tarot. I simply love how these cards capture and celebrate our soul's journey through life. The tarot deck is split into two parts: the minor arcana and the major arcana. The minor arcana has four suits of fourteen cards, ace to ten, with four face cards, King, Queen, Knight, and Page. The tarot deck has four suits that mirror the ancient Egyptian and Chinese playing cards from which the suits of diamonds, hearts, spades, and clubs originated. Each suit has an elemental equivalent.

- Clubs or wands, which began as batons or polo clubs, represent fire and our instincts and ideas.

- The hearts are represented by cups and the element of water offers insight into our ability to love, be loved, and share love.

- Spades evolved into swords in the tarot deck. These instruments reflect air and our intellect, and how the mind complements or interferes with our soul's evolution.

- Lastly, the diamonds are the suit of coins or more commonly pentacles. These circles with stars within reflect the earth and the lessons we learn surrounding our health and work, material gain and loss, money, and property.

My favorite part of the tarot is the major arcana. These twenty-two archetypes reflect our soul as "the Fool" journeying through the adventure of living within the physical world. Each card has so many layers of exploration you could spend a lifetime exploring their astrological, archetypical, numerological, elemental, and mythological origins and associations. The symbolism within the traditional pictures of the major arcana cards speaks to the history of all our souls upon this earth because each contains mystical and cultural influences from the Hebrew, Buddhist, Christian, Egyptian, Sufist, and Kabbalistic traditions.

Once the images and archetypes of the tarot were known to my soul, the spirit world began using them in my sittings. For example, although there is a Death card, whenever I would pull the Hangman card, it is an indication from the spirit world that there was a soul in spirit who wished to speak with my client.

To properly respect these cards, I would need to dedicate an entire book. They are great tools to help understand your soul, especially the major arcana because they can help you answer questions about yourself. It is difficult to read for yourself because it is hard to not desire a certain outcome; however, the tarot cards can help you gain objectivity.

Should you wish to explore these fantastic tools, here are a few suggestions. Because of their popularity, there are many decks to choose from. I am a traditionalist, so I feel that beginning with the Rider Waite deck is best because that deck captures the true archetypes and symbolism of the tarot.

When you first get a deck, fan out the cards in front of you face down. Start by rubbing your hands together for ten seconds like you did when you were sensing your energy field. Place your left hand, palm facing down, about three inches above the cards. Slowly run your hand over all the cards focusing upon the energy of your palm. Focus your attention on your soul feeling until you feel pulled to a card.

Once you have chosen a card, turn it over. Look within the card at the people, objects, colors, and their relationships to each other and the environment. How does it make you feel? Write down your observations. Your soul already speaks the symbolic language of the tarot. When you first buy a deck, try not to rely immediately upon the little white book, as it will feed your finite self with what the cards should mean to you. Instead let yourself discover the cards. Don't worry if you do not know what something is. You mind may not have the information, but your soul does. Try letting yourself explore the cards through your soul senses. If you listen to other ideas about the cards, you are discounting your own authentic response.

I also developed a deck of cards called the Divine Insight cards for anyone interested in learning to listen to their soul. Each deck has 47 picture cards and 13 color cards. There is no little white book defining the symbolism of each card, because I want you to discover their meaning to your soul. Therapists, counselors, readers, as well as intuitive beginners seem to enjoy the simple accessibility of my deck.

Whatever deck you use, let the journey be driven by your infinite self, whereby you do not need to be right, but rather discover the cards as new each time you use them. These are sacred tools, so treat them with love and respect. Some people place them in cloth, scarves, or in special boxes.

Pendulums

We have Galileo to thank for discovering the precision of the swing of a pendulum. Pendulums are wires or chains that have an attached weight or bob at one end. If you look inside a grandfather clock, you can see the pendulum swinging back and forth. For our purposes, pendulums are tools to help you sense energy and trust your soul senses and instincts. I have used them over maps to find a good location to move or to sense the energy movement of a chakra. Most pendulums you will find are quite attractive chains that have a tear-shaped stone or crystal hanging as the weight. If you take a pendulum and hold it above your hand, it will swing or move reflecting your thoughts. By simply dangling the pendulum motionless above a chakra, it will begin to mirror the energy movement within that energy center. Pendulums can spin clockwise or counterclockwise, move side to side, or sometimes be completely still. My suggestion is to just play with one. There are some Divine Spark pendulum exercises at the end of this chapter for you to experiment with.

Automatic Writing

Automatic writing can help you receive guidance and wisdom. What you are accessing is not your own thoughts within the finite self, but the voice of your infinite self and the universe. This is a great exercise to practice shifting out of the mind and into your soul, because you will begin to hear the differences between your thoughts and the voice of your soul.

To do this, begin with a prayer or dropping into your soul space. Have a pen and paper ready. Set an intention to receive wisdom from the universe and write a question in your journal. Take a deep breath in and release your question on the exhale. Keep your focus upon your breathing and just relax. You are not straining to hear, just surrendering to receive incoming guidance. Automatic writing is a flow of information. You can begin writing your question down over and over again until you begin to receive information. This practice takes patience and time. The more you commit to listening from your soul, the greater your return will be.

DIVINE SPARK EXERCISES:

In this chapter, we have focused on the ways you can consciously transmit to the universe, as well as ways to receive guidance and messages. Here are a few ideas to help you begin using these techniques to build bridges to and from the spirit world.

1. *Soul Recharging Visualization:* Record the soul recharging meditation described in this chapter and practice feeling the current of universal energy flowing through and around you. Creating a conscious connection to the spirit world, as well as a visual of how you recharge and release what no longer serves you, allows you to begin nurturing the energetic landscape of your soul.

99

2. *Month-Long Prayer Experiment:* Begin each day with a prayer for one person in your life. Do not let that person know you are praying for them. Witness the subtle changes that occur within your relationship, especially any shifts in how they act toward you. Do this experiment for at least one month. It is a great affirmation that what you are sending out returns in kind.

3. *Daily Intention Setting:* Begin each day setting a simple intention to honor your needs and your soul. Intentions are best worded in the present beginning with "I am." This vision can reflect something you are working on currently or support a desire you wish to manifest. Begin the day writing down your intention in a notebook. At the end of

the day, revisit your day for any synchronicities or validations of your soul desire manifesting.

4. *Sound Meditation Practice:* Practice listening to different environments and consciously not talking. You can practice this kind of mindfulness anywhere and have very different results. Sound meditations for relaxation and soul expansion are great outdoors, yet you can explore sound almost anywhere. Put on a favorite piece of music and really listen to each of the instruments. Tune into the sound inside of markets, stores, and offices, as each are calming in a different way. The act of practicing focused concentration has an automatically calming effect. As your soul senses become more sensitive, you will begin feeling the impact sound has upon your nervous system. Experiment and have fun with it.

5. *Daily Check-In:* In the morning, take a moment to think about the events of your day. Imagine each event, meeting, or encounter and check in with your soul senses. Do you get any initial impressions of what may transpire today? What do you hear, see, taste, touch, smell, feel, or know? Write down any sensations or visuals. At the end of the day, check in with your observations.

6. *Symbol Library:* To communicate with your soul, building an image dictionary can be very helpful. Write down any repetitive symbols, visuals, or impressions. The universe will help you build a library filled with shorthand visuals and symbols to help you understand the invisible language of your soul.

7. *Tarot Play:* Get a deck of tarot cards and pull out all the major arcana cards. Without looking at the little white book, just allow yourself to have your own relationship with the cards initially. Fan out all of the 22 cards and pick the card you are most drawn to as well as the card you like the least. Get out your journal and write down your impressions. Really spend time looking at the two cards and

discovering why your soul is drawn to one card and dislikes the other. For both cards, pick the person or thing you identify with most within the image and become it. Pretend you are stepping into the card. What do you notice looking to the right, left, up, down, behind you, and even out of the card back at you?

8. *Pendulum Exercise One:* Beyond the seven chakras in chapter 3, there are smaller chakras around the body. Within each palm are chakras which you can explore using a pendulum. Begin by holding the pendulum in your dominant hand while stilling the base or bob with your other hand until it ceases to move. Place your other hand's open palm a few inches below the pendulum's bob. While you focus upon your breath, the pendulum will begin to swing, naturally mirroring the energy movements of that hand's chakra. Notice how the pendulum moves. Is it circular? Which direction does it spin, clockwise or counterclockwise? You can also use your pendulum to check in when you experience different emotions and see how your life experiences are affecting your soul space. Once you've gotten a sense for using your pendulum to detect your own energy, you can expand your experiments to nature. Go outside and see what the pendulum does over a plant, a man-made object, or over a pet. Everything has energy and it is measurable, so enjoy.

9. *Pendulum Exercise Two:* You can use pendulums to check in with yourself as well. Hold the pendulum over your palm and say and think "yes." Allow the pendulum to reflect the energy of yes. Sometimes it may swing back and forth, move in a circle, or simply stand still. Repeat "yes" a number of times to make sure you know how the pendulum moves when you feel "yes." Now do the same exercise with "no." Notice how the pendulum moves differently. Once you establish a "yes" and "no," when you have a dilemma you need spiritual insight with, begin by centering yourself in

your soul. Next, ask for guidance that honors you and everyone involved for their highest good. Ask your question and see what the pendulum indicates. Practice makes perfect, but most of all, have fun.

In this chapter, you have explored the landscape of your own soul and the ways your soul transmits and receives guidance. In the next chapter, we are going to begin communicating with your own soul, as well as with those invisible guides who assist you along the way.

CHAPTER 6

Your Soul and Divine Guidance

We will recover our sense of wonder and our sense of sacred only if we appreciate the universe beyond ourselves as a revelatory experience of that numinous presence whence all things come into being. Indeed, the universe is the primary sacred reality. We become sacred by our participation in this more sublime dimension of the world around us.

—Thomas Berry

The first time I met Sophie was during a mediumship sitting. I was communicating with my client's mother in spirit, when a virtual giraffe sauntered into my office. She was as real as the client sitting across from me. My job is to relate what I receive, so I simply announced, "I have a giraffe joining you." It got a little tricky because both my client and the giraffe looked at me for clarity. My client was doe-eyed and unclear why a giraffe was with her, while Sophie simply leaned in, batting her long eyelashes. Sophie's presence did not feel literally connected to my client's spirit mom, in that she had not gone on a safari nor directly connected to giraffes in any way. But her mom was a huge animal lover who donated to numerous organizations that rescued and protected animals.

Over time, I discovered that Sophie is one of my guides. She celebrates human souls who honor the animal kingdom. Through the years, she has thanked my clients for rescuing feral cats, adopting animals, giving donations to animal shelters, and saving animals from adversity. I was in a sitting with a veterinarian when Sophie entered with a cow. This heifer thanked my client for saving her calf, as he had worked diligently to reposition her child within her womb. If I am sitting with someone who has contributed profoundly, Sophie will lick their cheek. She is delightful, entertaining, and deeply loving. My clients often respond by saying, "But that was so long ago." The animals do not have voices. They rely upon our kindness and awareness that they too inhabit this great earth. When such actions are demonstrated, trust me, they are noted. Sophie's presence fills my heart with joy and she has touched many of my clients. I simply cannot imagine working without her.

There are many invisible guides, teachers, and angels who work with and around us daily. Often, we do not recognize their presence, because we may not even know they are with us. These spirit beings offer guidance, support, and empower our soul. Although they cannot intervene, they can forewarn us of impending danger.

In my early twenties, I was living with a family whose mom was like a spiritual mentor to me. I was in the bathroom blow-drying my hair. As I was getting ready for work, a black cloudy mass sequentially shrouded each of the seven mirrors, one by one. The shadow being traveled quickly, but it certainly got my attention. When I told my second mom, she immediately insisted I was not to leave the house that day. She had an ominous feeling about what had transpired. I chose to go anyway.

It was one of the first true days of spring. I was in a van picking up supplies for the theatre department on Sunset Boulevard. I had the windows down, when my attention was diverted by a dog with its head stuck out a nearby car window. The car in front of me suddenly switched lanes to avoid a stalled flatbed truck. I didn't have time to react in the same way. I hit the truck going about 35 miles an hour.

The next thing I remember, I found myself standing in the back of the van. I have no idea how I got there. The van's windshield had popped out. I ended up with a few bruises, a mild concussion, and a boatload of embarrassment, but I was completely fine. The paramedics said numerous times how much worse my injuries should have been. At almost the exact moment of the accident, my spiritual mom called my boss and asked if I had returned from my runs.

The spirit world has helped me understand there are exit points: moments in our lives where we can potentially leave the physical world. I know with great certainty that day was one of mine. The dark energy being, who I initially responded to in fear, and my spiritual mom both were trying to help me avert the accident. I simply did not pay attention.

Guides and teachers have absolutely no personal agenda because their sole focus is to support us in our journey. Before we begin exploring these amazing beings, let's talk about how divine guidance feels and sounds.

UNDERSTANDING DIVINE GUIDANCE

Your spiritual entourage provides wisdom, support, healing, clarity, and inspiration throughout your life, although we are often unaware of their presence. Their voices and promptings are subtle, but if you have patience, tenacity, and commitment, you will find great value in developing relationships with these invisible guides.

Divine guidance is *received* much like an incoming text message, where the guidance just comes in without effort. You use your soul hearing to be open and available to their wisdom.

As your relationships build with your spiritual support team, you will become more aware of how your soul feels in their presence. They have a spiritual imprint, so you will recognize them within your soul space. Your soul senses will feel their powerful and focused authority, which can be intense, because they are more confident than we are in their prowess. You will feel safe in their presence. They are deeply invested in your soul and its evolution, so their communication style is always deeply respectful, supportive, and most of all, loving. They are with you especially in times of need, offering healing to your mind, body, emotions, and soul. They are in service to you.

The wisdom your soul hears is pure, concise, and applicable. Your guides' insight can be new information to help you gain clarity and inspiration or may affirm and confirm ideas you have or decisions you are making.

Your guides mainly utilize your soul senses of feeling, hearing, seeing, and knowing. For example, I could feel the dark energy in the mirror was intense; I could see it, and I knew it was significant

Divine guidance feels and sounds optimistic and hopeful. You will feel energized, renewed, peaceful, and balanced. You will never feel fear, only inspiration, love, and protection. Your guides can help you know when to do something, as well as when to avoid a situation. Their focus is only upon your highest good.

Years back, I was interested in doing an ayahuasca ceremony. Ayahuasca is a hallucinogenic plant, native to the Amazon, called the "vine of the dead." It is a very potent plant, as it takes your soul upon a very deep journey. I had a client whose brother became mentally unstable after such an experience and ended up taking his life, so I felt I had an adequate respect for what I was getting myself into. The night before the ceremony, I was awakened by a guide I had not met, standing next to my bed. I greeted him and asked his reason for coming. He simply asked me not to participate in the ceremony, as he indicated the facilitators could not vision my soul out of my body properly and it was potentially dangerous for me. Although I wanted to be a petulant child and argue, I knew it was for my own good. Working with your guides is very healing, as you will feel the power of their unconditional love.

Divine guidance is never mean, sarcastic, indifferent, disdainful, egocentric, or disrespectful. Your guides will not upset, threaten, complicate, control, discourage, blame, or dismiss you. They will never demand you do anything for them, especially not to harm another human being or yourself. They remind you just how important and loved your soul is.

YOUR SOUL SUPPORT TEAM

Your soul has many invisible guides and friends who support you in this physical journey. Some are constant companions who have eternal connections to you, while others are seasonal, circumstantial, or transitional guides. There are guides who support ideas and inventions, since these concepts are born in the universe first and then whispered to souls upon the earth. This is why someone releases a great invention and you may say, "That was my idea, too." Other guides are invested in helping humankind achieve equality, peace, and compassion. Some have walked upon this earth, while others exist only as spirit and represent a collective consciousness that informs humankind. Almost any pursuit you experience has some sort of virtual guidance system available to assist you in your becoming. If people could only understand how loved and supported they truly are, we could diminish loneliness if not eradicate it altogether.

This kind of support charges your soul by connecting to the energy and intelligence of the spirit world. Connecting to your guides is a great way to nurture yourself, because you are expanding your ability to sense and connect with what is invisible to the eye, but visible to the soul.

107

Archangels

I was deep in meditation one day when Paul Armitage's song "Angel Heart" unexpectedly began to play. Immediately, my soul began rising toward something unknown to me and as I floated upward, the weight of any feelings or thoughts that did not serve my soul fell away from me. I was guided above the clouds to a gateway and floated through the entrance. I found myself in front of a grand, illuminated being who radiated such a bright light that I could only engage in visual sips. I would glimpse a corner of a lip, swell of a cheek, or wave of hair. The being was much grander in scale than anything I had previously witnessed. Yet, the depth of unconditional love and immediate peace my soul felt streaming from this healing and miraculous presence remains with me to this day.

The luminous being I encountered in my meditation was the Archangel Gabriel. Archangels are the spiritual liaisons and messengers between humans and God. Each one's energy body is massive, so I often find their spiritual presence larger than the room I am in. I have often wondered if we commonly think they have wings because our soul sight witnesses the dynamic color and purity of their spirit.

The strong and loving presence of archangels guards this world, and they are available to each of us if we call on them. As intermediaries between our soul and spirit, they help us avoid potential outcomes that do not serve our soul, nurture our interests, and protect our becoming. Each has a unique energy presence, which reveals itself as your relationship grows. The archangels each connect to a specific element, as well as a compass direction which we will use to help you create an angelically held sacred space.

I want to focus on the four main archangels: Michael, Gabriel, Raphael, and Uriel. Should working with the angels resonate with your soul, there are many more archangels to explore. I have chosen these four because they work within my sacred space.

The archangels, like most guides and teachers, are invoked: you must request their presence. In doing so, you are empowering yourself to be worthy of such potent and graceful assistance. Like all guides, they cannot change what is happening, because that interferes with your free will. But they can help you make soul-centered decisions.

Archangel Michael: Described as "he who is like God," Archangel Michael is the most recognized and powerful angel. His sword is said to slay the dragons of our illusions so we can align with our personal empowerment. He represents the element of fire and the direction of the south. His protective presence allays your fear. Call on Archangel Michael when you wish to create an empowered and protected space.

Archangel Gabriel: The second highest archangel is Gabriel, often referred to as "the messenger and strength of God." He has dominion over the element of water and the west direction. He is the angel who heralds our souls with his trumpet, calling them to recognize what is unconscious within us so we can bring it into the light of spiritual awareness. He is often present when people embrace their spiritual nature by equally recognizing both the finite and infinite self. He balances mind and emotions so you can hear the greater truth of spirit. Additionally, he guards the babies coming into our world. Invoke Archangel Gabriel when you are completing life cycles and whenever you wish to hear spiritual messages and insights.

Archangel Uriel: The fire or light of God is Archangel Uriel. He represents the earth and the direction of the north. He guides us to recognize and love the polarity in all situations, including ourselves. He is the angel of creativity, so he reminds us there is a difference between the limited ideas of our mind and the unlimited potential of our soul. He helps transmute our guilt and shame so we can witness the greater gifts within situations. Call upon Archangel Uriel when you wish to spark your creativity or gain wisdom through objectivity.

109

Archangel Raphael: The healer of God is Archangel Raphael. His element is air and he aligns with the east direction. He helps heal our mind and body from addictive behaviors. His presence reminds us that illness and physical imbalance are often brought about when we are spiritually out of attunement. Call upon archangel Raphael to allow his unconditional love to flow within and around you.

One way to work with these angels is to invoke them where you meditate, spiritually explore, or work. They will fortify and surround your space with unconditional love and truly create a sacred space. Using a compass or app, create a direction grid for your space. Invoke Michael in the south, Gabriel in the west, Uriel in the north, and Raphael in the east. When you call them in, open your soul senses to perceive what you experience with each archangel. Perhaps you see Michael's sword or feel healing energy when Raphael enters. When you get flashes of color, refer to the color chart you made in chapter 4 and see how that archangel is working specifically with you. Just like any new relationship, the more time you spend with the archangels, the greater your awareness of them becomes.

Angels and Cherubs

Archangel Michael has told me that there are angels in every corner of every space upon the earth. Take a moment within the space you are in and envision that to be true. Every corner of the room has an angelic presence holding a loving space for the pure possibility of the world. Although there is a defined hierarchy in different traditions delineating angels to different assignments within the natural and supernatural worlds, their primary function is to infuse people, spaces, and places with love. We also have guardian angels who oversee our lives and remain connected to our soul. I will expand on this idea in the next chapter when we connect to our ancestors.

I simply adore cherubs. Cherubs appear to me as baby angels. If I am having a challenging day, I invoke the cherubs to come and play. They are always rosy-cheeked and silly, and their cute little baby bodies make me smile. They hold the same sweetness and purity that children exude. They just want to play and delight. I am immediately renewed anytime I ask them to join me.

Ascended Masters

Ascended masters are souls who once walked an enlightened path upon this earth, and instead of reincarnating, have chosen to remain in spirit to offer guidance to serve humankind. Much like the Greek pantheon has a number of Gods addressing different natural and personal needs, the masters have specific interests and abilities, as well as mastery of one aspect of human evolution. Some of the masters of spiritual living are Jesus, Buddha, Confucius, Mother Mary, Gandhi, and Mohammad. Each walked upon this earth as a human yet was able to allow their infinite self to guide their journey. They serve as spiritual inspirations and are deeply invested in our spiritual enfoldment because as we evolve, so does the universe.

There are legendary and historical masters like Merlin and King Arthur, and indigenous guides like White Buffalo Calf Woman, the Hawaiian goddess of the ocean Namahao Ke Ka'i, or the healing creation god of the Herero bushmen of Namibia, Mukuru. Yogi masters like Babaji and Paramanhansa Yogananda offer the benefits of meditation and personal insight.

In my home circle, where I sit with colleagues and blend with the spirit world, we have been graced by many ascended masters. I have been amazed how many times a number of us will witness the same master visiting and working with our group. Merlin worked with us for a time. His energy can be very direct and demanding. He seems to have little patience for dawdling. He required all of us to stand within our empowerment and meet his energy, which was thrilling.

I visited the Self-Realization Fellowship Temple in San Diego last year around the time of Paramanhansa Yogananda's birthday. I sat in for their bi-weekly meditation and felt his presence welcoming me. He began talking about future events in my life that absolutely came to fruition. He was gentle, loving, and carried tremendous wisdom.

111

I have also had amazing encounters with Jesus. The first time I sensed his soul, I was doing an energy healing on a beautiful young girl whose heart had been challenged a great deal within her life. I witnessed Jesus descend above her, reach into her energy body, and replace her heart with his. It was such an innocent and stunning gesture of love. I chose not to share what had transpired with my client, as I was uncertain of her religious beliefs. Upon leaving my office, she stopped and said, "Austyn, this is amazing—I feel like I have a new heart." I wonder if the "second" coming of Jesus occurs when we create a personal connection to his soul and let him teach us how to love unconditionally.

The ascended masters are great guides to help you explore your soul. Since each represents a very different discipline and gift, you can call in a master who aligns with your life. Be open to who appears. If working with these wisdom keepers appeals to you, please take the time to explore and discover. Who knows what insight Neptune, Isis, or Oshun may have to offer you.

Personal Guides and Teachers

Each of us has personal spirit guides who choose to work with our individual soul. Some stay with us for our entire lifetime upon the earth, while others are more seasonal and escort us through specific times, lessons, and endeavors. These guides can be from different cultures and parts of the world. What differentiates these guides from others is that they work specifically and personally with your soul. These are the guides that you can connect to and develop profound relationships with. Sophie is such a guide for me. As your friendship with them deepens, you will be amazed at the way they can help you. To deepen your soul conversations, you can practice automatic writing, mentioned in the last chapter.

Guides can introduce themselves in meditations, dreams, and visions. I encourage you to discover your guides on your own, rather than asking someone to tell you who your guides are. These are very intimate relationships and you are fully capable of discovering their presence simply by asking for them to make themselves known to you. When you become aware of such a guide, you may realize you have known them all along. Your guides are working in the background of your life already, so you will not need to go very far to discover their presence.

Channels are people who allow a spirit guide to use their physical body to communicate. I have seen a few powerful channeling demonstrations. But be forewarned, some people demonstrate how channeling can go wrong when there is more ego than spiritual presence. In these cases, individuals are in their finite self and think they are representing the spirit realm. When seeking out these experiences, please use your discernment and remember the guidelines for divine guidance. Channeled wisdom should inspire and expand your awareness, and offer new information, not just evoke a personality who pretends to be your next guru.

An excellent example of channeling is author and inspirational speaker Esther Hicks. She channels Abraham, a group of evolved nonphysical teachers, and has inspired audiences all over the world since 1986. Collective consciousnesses are groups of souls and spirits who work together to manifest the same potential upon the earth. Esther would not be able to grace us with their wisdom if she had not deeply surrendered and allowed Abraham's spirit to infuse her petite physical body and inform her soul. Esther did not seek Abraham; rather, he began working with her and her now-deceased husband Jerry. What transpired changed the focus of both of their lives and has added great value to millions. Together they have published over 700 books and audio productions empowering individuals to communicate with spirit so they can abundantly cocreate joyful lives.

Spirit Doctors

Many souls deeply study and investigate the human body and become masters of their trade during their lifetime. Their passion for understanding healing and medicine can also follow them in the spirit world. If their soul chooses, they may act as spirit doctors who assist the future evolution of doctors, physical healing, and the application of medicine upon the earth. Some guides incarnate to learn medicine and practice it in the physical world, so they can be of deeper assistance guiding us in spirit.

Spirit doctors generally work as a collective consciousness like Abraham, because there is an expanded potential and power when many souls focus upon a single intent. The only times I have witnessed an individual spirit doctor making his or her presence known is when I am working with a medium who wishes to develop their medical intuition. Medical intuitives are able to use their soul senses to specifically perceive information that benefits the physical health of their clients, as most view the body as an X-ray. It is a very specific talent that often develops in individuals who are already interested in medicine and have a thorough understanding of the human body.

I was recently teaching a group of developing mediums and prior to a class, almost a quarter of them reached out the night before saying they might need to cancel due to a cold or the flu. In our opening meditation, I asked the spirit doctors to work with each of us to release what no longer served us and align our bodies with

113

dynamic health. We all felt their subtle presence within and around us. As the weekend progressed, the students all felt remarkably better.

The spirit doctors are great to call in to empower an upcoming surgery, a surgical team, or any medical issue or concern you are experiencing. When you call them in, pay particular attention to your soul feeling, as you may feel subtle energies within your body shifting. Audio for the following practice that calls upon your spirit doctors is available at http://www.newharbinger.com/41849.

✴ EXERCISE ✴
Healing with Spirit Doctors

You may wish to have some peaceful music playing. Make sure you are physically comfortable, so you will not be distracted. Begin by calling in the angels to create your sacred space. Sit upright in a chair and ask the spirit doctors to empower your physical body to align with your soul and restore you to perfect health. Allow at least five minutes for this healing. While you are sitting there, pay attention to your soul feeling and keep your awareness within your soul space. You may feel tingles, warmth, cold, or become aware of certain parts of your body. When you finish, thank the spirit doctors and release the angels.

Each guide you work with will feel and appear differently. Listen to your soul feeling, knowing, hearing, and sight. You are practicing receiving energy when working with guides and teachers.

Your Infinite Self

The final guide and teacher I wish to talk about is perhaps the most significant relationship for you to develop. This guide is with you through eternity, and is your infinite self. The wisdom of your own soul is profound. This relationship connects you with your most pure and divine essence. We can often give credit to our guides and teachers, but ultimately, we possess incredible wisdom and insight because we are part of the infinite intelligence of the universe. To look within and develop the relationship with your own higher wisdom is imperative. In fact, it is my hope that this book offers you many ways you can wander upon the invisible path of your soul and trust your own innate insights.

YOUR SPIRITUAL ROUND TABLE

In chapter 5, we did a meditation where light infused our soul space. We began visualizing a pool of light above that entered our crown chakra through a funnel. One day I imagined rising up through my crown chakra and into the funnel that connected me to the energy of the universe. Surrounding the opening of the funnel, I witnessed a round table of my key guides, angels, teachers, and souls invested in my soul's evolution, seated much like King Arthur's knights. What follows is a meditation inspired from my experience that will help you meet your core guides. Audio for this practice is available at http://www.newharbinger.com/41849.

❋ EXERCISE ❋
Meet Your Round Table Guides

Find a place and space where you feel comfortable, safe, and will not be disturbed. If you play music, make sure it is pleasant and not distracting. Open sacred space by calling in the archangels. Close your eyes and become aware of your breath. Follow the breath as you inhale, filling your lungs, and exhale gently out of your mouth. On the next inhale, follow the breath as it enters your nose, goes down your throat, and fills your lungs. Hold the air in your lungs for three seconds and slowly exhale out of the mouth. Repeat this a few times until you feel your body begin to relax.

Imagine you are "little you" standing on top of your head: perfect, playful, ready to explore. Take a moment to witness how "little you" is today. Feel your soul space extending out all around, above, and below you. Slowly look up and witness a spinning funnel of light connecting your soul space to the universe. Watch as the funnel-like energy spins above you. That chakra gets brighter and brighter until it illuminates the entire space of your soul, surrounding you in loving white light. You feel yourself begin to rise up, up, up to the top of your soul space. You rise into that funnel of loving energy above your head that connects to the universe. Watch as the energy expands to spin around you. The light is healing, relaxing, and rejuvenating. You feel your soul rising into this space, as your soul feeling, hearing, seeing, and knowing deeply open and expand. Open and expand.

You arrive at the top of the funnel and witness below you the spinning light spiraling into your physical body below. As you look around, realize you have arrived at the top of that vortex. Below you is your physical body and all around you is spirit. Become aware of a circle of light swirling around you. The light begins to form a donut-shaped table. You are in the middle space, with a circular table around you.

This is the round table where you can meet your guides. You are in the center of the table with four guides present. One is directly in front of you in the position of north. Each guide is 90 degrees right of the other, so there is a guide for each cardinal direction. With your soul feeling, seeing, hearing, and knowing, perceive their collective presence. Each sends you a beam of light that illuminates your soul with unconditional love. Take a moment to receive their love and witness the light.

"Little you" floats off of your head and lands in the chair across the round table, directly in front of you in the direction of the north. Witness as "little you" transforms into your infinite self. You are now sitting across from your pure spiritual essence. Using your soul feeling, bridge your soul's energy into the purity of your infinite self. Feel the unconditional love and healing connecting with your divine essence. What does your infinite self look like? Use your soul senses to perceive any colors, feelings, visuals, and sounds. Simply allow yourself to explore and perceive. Take a deep breath in and exhale.

Shift your attention 90 degrees to the right of your infinite self, to the direction of the east and the next guide seated at your round table. Stepping forward to fill that space is the archangel working most closely with your soul. Drop into your soul feeling and perceive who is there. Perhaps you will see Michael's sword, Gabriel's trumpet, feel healing energy from Raphael, or observe the fire and love from Uriel. Relax into your awareness and allow the images, sensations, and feelings to fill the space between you and your archangel. Sense into that space and feel the exchange of unconditional love. Witness your archangel's looming, powerful presence. Luxuriate in their love for a few moments.

Shift your awareness another 90 degrees to the south direction to become aware of the next guide who guards your soul. Seated directly opposite your infinite self at the table is one of your ancestors who works most closely with your soul. Simply release the need to know and surrender to your senses. Allow your ancestor to fully materialize before you. Using your soul feeling, how does it feel to be reunited with their soul? What do they wish to say to you? What do you wish to say to them? Spend a few minutes in their loving company. When you are ready, take a deep breath in and exhale.

Finally, shift your attention to your left and witness an ascended master or master guide joining your table. This figure may be known or unknown to you. Allow him or her to fully materialize before you and be open to receiving impressions with your soul senses. Become curious about all that you can perceive. Is the figure a man or a woman? Young or old? How are they dressed? What are they wearing on their feet? What can you see, feel, or hear? You may have an immediate picture or simply sense their presence. Relax and allow your soul to be in their presence. Using your soul feeling, imagine a beam of light extending from your solar plexus to theirs. Ask for guidance. Is there any object on the table in front of the master? If so, what is it? Just relax and notice. Take a deep breath in and exhale.

Explore each direction and revisit each guide. In the north, your infinite self. In the east, your archangel. In the south, your ancestor, and in the west, your ascended master or guide. Allow each of them to recharge, restore, and renew you to perfect heart-centeredness and radiance. They may send beams of light into your soul space. When they have recharged you, ask what your guides know to be true about you that you have forgotten. Receive their messages, love, and wisdom. Take your time.

When you have received their insight, thank your guides for their love and healing. Return your focus to the round table and the circle of light around you. Witness how your guides transition into the light of the circle around you. Slowly begin to descend, coming back, back into your soul space. Feel your soul distill into your head, neck, shoulders, arms, torso, hips, legs, and feet until you are fully returned to your body. Take a deep breath in and exhale. When you are ready, open your eyes. If you wish, take a few minutes to write down your observations in your journal. The round table meditation is a simple exercise that gives you a place and space to work with your guides. Please do not be discouraged if one or more of your guides was not evident to you. Simply rejoice in what you were able to perceive.

118

Just like you seek out a friend for support, you can reach out and work with your guides. When you are speaking, you are transmitting your wishes and desires. Spirit communication with guides, masters, or ancestors is a two-way communication. Simply focus on your breathing anytime your finite self begins to wonder or comment on your progress. Just allow your soul senses to receive. You can return to the round table and ask for wisdom and messages.

Guides and teachers are like any friendship: they require investment, commitment, and communication. Your spiritual support team is meant to complement your journey, so honor them with your trust, time, and love. The more you sit in sacred space and allow their wisdom to be received, the more profound your life will become. You will be amazed at their observations and wisdom.

DIVINE SPARK EXERCISES

The following exercises will help you get to know and practice working with your spirit support team: your infinite self, archangel, spirit guide, and ascended masters.

1. *Journaling:* Get out your journal and answer questions from this chapter. When have you been divinely guided? How was the round table meditation for you? What was it like to witness "little you" becoming your infinite self? Which of your guides, archangels, spirit guides, and ascended masters could you most easily connect with? Which guides require more investigation? Which of your soul senses was most powerful during the meditation?

2. *Research:* Follow your curiosity to research your ascended master, spirit guide, and archangel. There are many books and articles online. Just let your discernment parent your curiosity.

3. *Establish an Energy Language:* You have used a pendulum to sense a "yes" and "no." Drop into your soul, feeling and thinking of something that you absolutely agree with. It may be a person, situation, or circumstance. Once you have picked something, simply focus upon it and see how "yes" feels within and around you. Take a deep breath in and exhale, releasing the yes energy. Now focus upon something you absolutely disagree with. Drop into your soul feeling and sense where the energy of "no" exists within and around you. Inhale and exhale, releasing the no energy. You have now established an energy "yes" and "no." From now on, you can check in with your infinite self before making decisions

and see if you get an energy impression from your infinite self. You are developing an energy language, so this takes practice and time.

4. *Seek Guidance:* Get out your journal and write down a question for which you would like guidance. Repeat the beginning of the round table meditation and arrive standing in the center of your table, with your guides sending their light to your soul. Turn to face the direction of your guide or angel and open your soul hearing to receive insight regarding your question. Allow each guide to start with an inspirational word or phrase to assist you. Write down what you hear. Perhaps you will see colors, visuals, or feelings. This practice of soul listening, receiving, and writing is a great way to strengthen your relationships with your support team.

5. *Create Visuals:* Get out crayons, pens, pencils, or markers and draw your round table guides. Drawing can enhance the visuals, so you may find as you draw you will notice even more details.

Now that you have practiced soul perceiving and receiving with your spiritual support team, you are ready to connect with some of the souls most known to you in the spirit world: your ancestors and pets.

CHAPTER 7

Soul-to-Soul Communication

I don't want to have lived in vain like most people. I want to be useful or bring enjoyment to all people, even those I've never met. I want to go on living even after my death!

—Anne Frank

A woman came to see me who had lost all sense of the value of her life and was not sure if she wished to remain living. Unsure about the afterlife, she asked me questions about mediumship and suicide. Over the next few months, we exchanged emails and she grew to trust me. Since she was deciding if she wanted to "leap" into the other world, her nickname was "Frog."

Months later at an evening mediumship demonstration, I connected with a man from spirit named Mark. He had been a police officer and was looking for his best friend. I connected his soul to a small-framed woman with dark hair in the back of the room. When she stood up, I realized it was Frog. She looked simply terrified. Mark named mutual work colleagues and friends, shared memories of vacations in the woods, and even congratulated her on the new truck. He clearly had been like a brother to her. She had never mentioned him to me, but his absence in her life was part of the reason she had lost hope.

In a moment between his thoughts, a single sound emerged from a muted cell phone in the row in front of Frog. Everyone heard it. It was a sound the phone's owner later validated she did not even know existed. The sound was a frog's ribbit. Frog and I simply stared at each other, transfixed. Clearly, Mark needed her to understand he knew what she had been considering. It was an impeccably-timed intervention from Mark's soul that affirmed his love. He was helping Frog understand that it was not her time. It was a big sign, one she could not deny.

Mark's presence had a great influence on Frog. She reengaged in life and was doing great when she found out she had cancer. It was a grand test, and Frog fought hard for her life which she had previously wished to release. I am happy to say Frog survived and has been cancer-free for more than eight years!

A great joy in my job comes from stories like this. I am over-whelmed by the love our family, friends, and pets share with us once they transition. Whether it be through signs, messages, or making their presence known, their desire is to comfort and love. Healing is the most powerful gift imparted by mediumship, because we fre-quently forget the value of our soul and our life. We get lost, afraid, overwhelmed, and sad. We feel disempowered all too frequently by the events of the world. We can be left with a myriad of emotions, the least of which is helplessness. I marvel at the efforts and desire of the spirit world to help us get through our lives.

You are blessed to have souls who remember your truth, and they are a thought away. You have met your guides, so now it is time to spend some time with the human and animal souls who have loved you. Your spirit family must also follow the guidelines for divine guidance outlined in the last chapter. They can offer guid-ance, support, recognize your actions, and congratulate your becom-ing. They love to talk about what has happened in the physical world since they died to affirm their soul is always with you. They some-times recognize new souls coming into our world or souls who have transitioned to the spirit world. They speak of shared memories and what they loved. They will mention family events and celebrations, as well as acknowledge your challenges to affirm their support.

However, they have new rules upon transitioning out of their body. The main change for them is they have become a witness to life and no longer a participant. They are not all knowing. They are still evolving as they were when they were alive. No matter how challenging or abusive the relationship you had with them was on earth, they cannot harm or insult you further. They cannot foretell the future, or tell you what to do. They have had their opportunity to live and now it is your turn. Although their personality will be evident, they are not tethered to their finite self. By transitioning to their infinite self, they understand that their unfinished business is their sole responsibility, which can inspire their desire to connect with you.

The spirit world made me realize just how important healing can be. Just like I did not understand the reason for Sophie's presence, I will often be shown something during a sitting that confounds me. One day, I was doing a reading for a young man. The spirit world showed me his dad, along with his paternal grandfather and great-grandfather, all shackled at the ankles. At first, my mind assumed they had all been imprisoned, but as I took that idea to my soul senses, I realized that visual was the way the spirit world was telling me that things ran in the family. I was being shown that alcoholism was not only in his family but connected back three generations. During our sitting, this young man's father acknowledged he was aware his son was not only sober, but was a sponsor for other souls working through the program. At this moment, I witnessed all of the ankle irons connecting the three generations click open and drop out of sight. I also felt with my soul a huge emotional release. As I looked at my client, he was tearing up. He apologized, as he did not understand the suddenness of his emotion. What I came to realize was this young man had shifted the soul pattern within his family because he had dealt with the addiction consciously. All it took was for one soul to take on the generational pattern for it to shift. Not only had he freed his soul, the unfinished business related to alcohol from the prior three generations had equally shifted, which was represented by the ankle irons releasing.

123

When any soul, whether in spirit or upon this earth, becomes accountable for their actions, the entire soul family or group can advance into new experiences because those on earth no longer need to repeat the same pattern. Mediumship also creates a potential opportunity for souls in the spirit world to be accountable.

Before we step into ways to connect with your loved ones in the spirit world, I wish to address some misperceptions regarding energy and the spirit world. I have been blessed to indulge my curiosities by deeply investigating, learning, practicing, and working with clients for more than three decades. To truly be of service, I had to figure out what I believed. I needed to learn from my own experiences and practices, as well as integrate the wisdom I was gaining from the souls in the spirit world.

I gathered what I had been taught and knew and analyzed, dismissed, refined, and arrived at an authentic cosmology I could stand behind. This is the approach I encourage you to embrace. No matter where you gain information, honor your soul enough to accept only what feels right, regardless of the opinions of others.

To be an authority on any subject is a lifelong discipline. Give yourself permission to question everything and come to your own conclusions. I do not offer these ideas to tell you what is real. I can only share what makes sense to me. If your aspiration is to always learn and grow, beliefs should equally evolve. Your life experiences, spiritual path, upbringing, cultural exposures, and what others have told you shape your beliefs about the spirit world and energy. I have deep respect for your beliefs. I only want to assist you in exploring your cosmology by offering my observations.

COMMON QUESTIONS ABOUT SOULS AND THE AFTERLIFE

Pop-culture versions of the afterlife favor sensationalism and drama, so it can be difficult to discern the truth about souls in spirit. What follows are questions I receive frequently that deserve our respect.

Are There Evil Spirits?

Evil does not exist in the spirit realm. Unfortunately, it does exist in the physical world, because it is a creation of humankind. Humans can be evil toward ourselves and each other. Evil is the darkest part of the finite self. When we allow ourselves to hate, murder, fight, and destroy, we are clearly disconnected from our infinite self. Our experience upon this earth is to understand the finite self, or the power of our mind. As long as our finite self operates without a spiritual awareness, we will always know evil. As humans, we tend to project our experience upon what we do not understand. Therefore, since we know evil, we will incorrectly assume spirit is evil. This is a fear-based assumption which comes from the finite self. Fear does not indicate the presence of something evil. As we discovered in the last chapter, the spirit world has many guides and helpers who have great authority and presence, which is very powerful but is not to be feared. We must always investigate what we feel.

Recently I had a discussion with a young lady. She told me a demon wanted to suck out her soul. The Latin word for demon simply means "spirit," so I was curious how she defined that word. She related it to the dementors in the *Harry Potter* series. As we talked more, she revealed that a dark, shadowy energy often came to her at times in her life when she was afraid or about to embark upon a great adventure. She simply assumed that because it was dark, it was evil and indicated impending danger, so she naturally feared its presence. Through the course of our conversation, she realized the demon had always been present when she was scared. We did a little guided work for her to encounter that being. She realized he had been a guide all along. Her fear prevented her from seeing his benevolence. Because he was dark and incredibly strong, she misinterpreted his intentions.

Many have been taught through religions that evil spirits exist and can overpower us. The finite mind will believe this, because our minds and emotions create fear. Because we do not own the fullness of our own power, we can believe others have power over us. The

125

finite self does not acknowledge a power greater than its own, so it will assume that a dark force is evil.

Within mediumship sittings, even souls who had evil intentions or were unkind to others during their life on earth are never malicious to the souls they are communicating with. If they were disrespectful or had abusive tendencies during their physical life, upon their physical death, they can gain objectivity. Without the input of the finite self, their soul can objectively look at their earthly experiences to gain awareness regarding the impact of their deeds, actions, and thoughts. This replay of their life allows their soul to feel the experience of others to understand the impact of their actions.

Once a soul dies, they do not have power to destroy or damage us in any way, as they are now observers to this world instead of participants. Some are inspired to acknowledge their actions. Not all souls will accept accountability. For some, it is just not within the scope of their soul's current evolution. Although they may not have the words to express their remorse, I often feel it within their soul. This is not something a medium should ever force, because mediums will equally be held accountable for all we say during our sittings. Our job is solely to translate what we receive.

We incarnate to play roles and gain empathy for ourselves and others, so there will be souls upon this earth who do not act with respect until we regain the balance between our finite and infinite selves. The spiritunity is to embrace personal responsibility now in all areas of your life, so your soul's contribution enhances the evolution of the future souls upon the earth.

What Are Hauntings?

We are used to thinking of our self as a physical being. Since we understand physical things exist in only one place, we cannot conceive of being in multiple places at once. Although this is physically correct, it is not true for our soul. When I was five and the runway appeared next to me, I was conscious of being in two places with equal awareness in both. How often are you talking to one person and also thinking of your child, spouse, or a friend? It is possible for our soul to be in multiple places at the same time and not be diminished. Hauntings are souls in spirit revisiting their lives and experiences. These souls are not stuck, just reconnecting to a place and time that is familiar to them.

When we talk about a memory and have a vivid picture of its surroundings within our mind, a part of our soul is revisiting that location by traveling in both time and space. I think that some of the people we see as ghosts are nothing more than souls remembering and time traveling. When we die, we are no longer physical and our soul can travel anywhere. Wouldn't you want to return to places that were meaningful in your life?

Do Souls Get Stuck?

Souls don't get stuck, we do. The idea of being "stuck" is a mental concept of the finite self. One way we get stuck is in our finite self's fear of death. The spirit of our soul is light energy, which is always in motion. Therefore, our soul cannot get stuck, no matter what happens to us at death. Once our physical body dies, our soul transitions back to spirit. Other souls, both alive and in the spirit world, are present for our transition out of our body. What does get stuck are our thoughts, emotions, and memories from being on earth. These are "imprints," which are often misinterpreted as stuck souls.

127

What Are Imprints?

Have you ever walked into a room after someone has had a fight and grown anxious? The discomfort that your soul feeling was perceiving was an imprint. Imprints are energy leftovers from impactful human emotions, thoughts, or actions within a space.

When I visited Auschwitz, I was filled with uncertainty and trepidation about what I would experience. When it first came into view, the grounds had just been blanketed in snow. I was mentally thrown, because it looked peaceful. As I released my fear and simply asked to experience the grounds anew, I was surprised when one of my first perceptions was grace. Although the atrocities that occurred there were massive, our world has gained great insight, respect, and compassion for the individuals whose lives were altered or ended at Auschwitz. I expected to feel human suffering, yet I also felt the results of love and prayers sent from around the world toward those souls and that place. If I had not opened up to the possibility that there was more than just the stories I had been told, I would have missed sensing the healing power that love can have upon a place over time.

Unfinished aspects of our life remain within this world as imprints to inform future generations. Because we incarnate to progress our soul, as well as those connected to us, when we have unfinished business upon our death, those feelings and thoughts also remain within this physical dimension. Think of the phrase "What happens in Vegas, stays in Vegas." Issues that were not resolved remain to shape the experiences of future souls, because the goal is always evolution.

Your soul can either enhance or diminish the human potential by how you choose to live your life, but equally by how willing you are to be accountable. You do not need to be perfect, just open to growing and learning from your life and the choices you make.

PREPARING TO CONNECT TO YOUR LOVED ONES IN SPIRIT

The souls in the spirit world wish nothing more for you than to enjoy your life and feel triumphant about how it unfolds. Their support and love are constant and available to you, always. Before I lead you through exercises to connect with ancestors and loved ones, let's review preparation techniques.

Always Connect Within Sacred Space

Before any spiritual exercise, please allow time to consciously shift from your finite self to your infinite self. The transition to your infinite self is key before doing any work in this book. Once you have opened to communicate with your soul, you can do multiple exercises, but always make sure you open and close your soul space when you finish connecting to the universe.

You can create sacred space by calling in your compass angels. You can also work with your round table guides by calling in your infinite self, archangel, spirit guide, and ascended master to honor your soul space. Once you are aware of their presence, drop your attention into your soul seat. Take a few deep breaths. Intend to be of service to your soul, the souls connected to you, and the spirit world. You can use the Opening to Receive meditation in chapter 5 as well. At this point, you will be in the right space for your soul senses to perceive and receive.

SOUL IMPRESSIONS

Each of us has an energetic impression much like our fingerprint that uniquely identifies our soul. As you connect with loved ones in spirit, you will want to invite each to help you sense their unique soul within your aura. By becoming aware of what distinguishes one soul from another, you can begin to sense and identify them whenever they are present. As much as I think of my spirit loved ones, I am always so very touched when I sense their souls with me, as they can miss me, too.

For some, the impact our pets have upon our soul is greater than any human relationship. We allow ourselves to unconditionally love our pets, so their loss can be quite profound. This exercise can be used to sense both your loved ones and pets in spirit. I suggest starting with a pet, as most people easily perceive their souls. If you haven't had a pet, ask for an animal you may have met or known to work with you. Audio for this practice is available at http://www.newharbinger.com/41849.

❋ EXERCISE ❋
Soul Sensing Your Pet

Find a space within your home or office where you can sit a foot away from a blank wall. Close your eyes, become comfortable, and simply focus upon your breath. Witness and follow the breath as it comes in and releases from your body. Do this three times. Transmit a thought to the spirit world that you are ready to work.

Expand your awareness into your soul space. Imagine your soul extends a few feet in front, to the right, behind, above, and below you. Relax into the space. Once that space is defined, ask for a pet in spirit connected to your soul to appear in front of you just outside your soul space. You do not need to ask for a specific pet, just see which one shows up. It will be as if your pet is looking at you through a window.

Using your soul senses, begin to perceive their energy in front of you using your soul sight, hearing, feeling, knowing, taste, touch, and smell. Each of your senses will more deeply connect you to your pet.

When you are ready, ask your pet to come into your soul space and let you feel where they wish to create their soul impression. Just release the request and focus upon your breathing. Witness as your pet stands, sits, or floats into a location within your soul space. It can be anywhere around your body, by your feet, to your side, or perhaps around your shoulder. Perhaps you feel tingling or their energy body resting against yours. Relax and just feel. Perceive where your pet creates their soul print. Whatever you perceive is perfect.

Once you can sense your pet, ask them to step outside your soul space. Feel into the space where they were to affirm they have stepped out. Now ask them to return to validate their spot. Notice where their soul returns. The goal is to observe where they choose to be within your soul space. Repeat inviting them into and releasing them from your soul space to affirm their chosen position. When you are satisfied, call them back in and have some love time. Thank them, share love, and then release their soul back to spirit.

✺

CREATING A VIRTUAL PLACE IN YOUR SOUL SEAT

Now that you have felt a soul within your soul space, let's spend some time with our loved ones in spirit. The following is a meditation to help you create a new virtual location within your soul seat to meet and spend time with your spiritual loved ones. Audio for this meditation is available at http://www.newharbinger.com/41849.

✺ MEDITATION ✺
Visiting the Ancestor Tree

You can work with your ancestor tree within your soul space any time you wish to connect with your spirit loved ones. You can visit pets, relatives, and friends. This tree is always there for you as a place of healing and remembrance within the seat of your soul.

Imagine "little you" standing on the top of your head. Directly in front of you is an elevator. Let the doors of the elevator open. Step in and turn around to face the doors as they begin to close. Push the button that takes you to the seat of your soul.

When the doors open, you find yourself stepping onto grass in an open field. In the distance is the most beautiful tree. Its trunk is strong and its branches reach out like arms holding sunlight. It is warm and inviting. You move toward the tree. You can see the light glistening on the leaves, and watch the gentle breeze animating the branches. Standing beneath its limbs, you notice the veins of the leaves illuminated with sunlight. You feel calm and relaxed.

The tree's trunk is solid and strong. You follow it down to the earth and witness a pair of shoes resting against the trunk. They belong to a loved one you know in the spirit world. Allow the shoes to fully materialize. Using your soul sight, what do they look like? What color are they? Observe what you can. The shoes begin to move and walk forward, stopping directly in front of you. The soul connected with those shoes begins to appear before you and animate. Witness as they form legs, hips, torso, arms, neck, and head. Look into this person's soul and take in a breath together. Welcome your loved one. Do not worry if you only see a part of them materialize, just trust what happens.

Knowing they have chosen this moment to connect with you, ask them: "Why have you come forward today?" Ask the question within your soul, release the need to know, and open your soul senses to receive their answer.

When they finish, ask them: "What can I learn from your soul?" Breathe and receive their answer.

Finally, ask them: "What do you know about me that I have forgotten?" Breathe and receive. Now spend whatever time you wish with their soul. Should there be any unfinished business between you, simply allow that healing to take place. You can imagine any residual feelings or memories that do not serve you simply falling away and absorbing into the earth below.

When you have finished your visit, thank their soul and watch them walk behind the tree to return to pure spirit. Take in the view of your tree and notice if anything has changed since your arrival. Thank the tree for holding a sacred space. Walk back across the open field to where you began standing on the grass. When you are ready, see the elevator. Step in, turn around, push the top button. When you arrive, the doors open and you step out. Take a deep breath in and exhale. When you are ready, open your eyes.

✳

DEEPENING YOUR ABILITY TO SENSE THE SPIRIT WORLD

To deepen your ability to connect to the spirit world is a grand adventure into your soul. It is a shift from thinking to sensing which requires a different kind of listening. One technique that greatly helped me was to create a space where I could really focus upon how the energy around me felt. For this purpose, I use a cabinet. Imagine a three-walled closet with a top, and instead of a door there is a curtain. Mediums sit in these boxes and go into deeper levels of meditation or trance. Most mediums are mental mediums, named this because the spirit world uses their mind and soul senses to communicate. Physical mediums allow the spirit world to animate and use their physical body. They have a rare and unique talent to create a substance called ectoplasm. The medium goes into a deep sleep-like trance and the spirit world creates this membrane-like substance, ectoplasm, that emerges from a physical medium's nose, mouth, or ears. Spirit blends into that substance to create a physical form through which a spirit can communicate or temporarily occupy space. There are amazing spirit photographs of physical mediums with fully-manifested spirit faces, bodies, or objects emerging from the ectoplasm that were perfectly visible to the eye. There are stories of spirits coming through the ectoplasm and physically appearing as they did in life.

My husband made me a spirit cabinet. It is spectacular—and it breaks down in moments, so I can travel easily with it. My desire is not necessarily to develop as a physical medium. Rather, my cabinet is a fabulous way for my students to truly feel spirit's energy within their soul space. They can call in their pet or loved one and really feel their soul.

When I taught a mediumship class on the Queen Mary in Long Beach, I brought my cabinet inside the Churchill Suite. As a small red light shone upon the faces of the mediums seated inside, we were amazed at what we witnessed. We saw "spirit eyes." This phenomenon happens when the physical eyes of the sitter in the cabinet are closed, but the soul in spirit's are open, so it looks like they are watching and looking. This may sound scary, but honestly, it is simply amazing. These spirit eyes looked all around the room. We saw transfigurations, which is when a person's face seems to completely physically alter in appearance or gender. We witnessed a woman morphing into a man with a beard, a man appearing as a woman 30 years his senior, and one woman disappearing almost entirely as the soul of a very young boy took her place. The souls aboard the Queen Mary were yet again visible and we were thrilled to witness them.

You can create a similar space by finding a corner of a room and putting a rod across the adjoining walls to form a sort of triangular closet. Drape fabric from the rod to enclose the space. You can also make a cabinet frame out of PVC piping and cover it with fabric or a sheet. Creating this sacred space is peaceful and will deepen your ability to sense the spirit world and souls around you.

After creating your cabinet, open sacred space with a prayer or loving intention and sit with Spirit. Within such a contained space, you can truly feel the space of your soul. I find these moments are best without any music. Allow your soul senses to expand into the space. Set an intention to blend your soul with the spirit world.

THE POTENTIAL OF MEDIUMSHIP

I wish to finish the chapter celebrating two gentlemen who inspire me to keep hope and positive expectations for the future of mediumship and interdimensional communication.

Perhaps the greatest physical medium ever was the famous English trance and direct voice medium Leslie Flint. Imagine what it would be like to not only get messages from your loved ones, but to actually hear their voices speaking to you. English trance and independent direct voice medium Leslie Flint had such a talent. To produce spirit voices, ectoplasm would form into a voice box outside of his physical body through which spirit voices could speak. People who attended his events could hear the actual voice of their deceased love ones speaking to them. Because this ability was so unique, he was tested by many people and organizations. To prove the voices were not coming from his mouth or larynx, he would sit within a cabinet where he was bound and often had his mouth covered. This may sound extraordinary, but he voluntarily submitted to such treatment to validate the authenticity of his work. Sometimes he was asked to hold colored water in his mouth for an entire session, as well as have a microphone to register vibrations from his larynx. People who witnessed his talent could have no doubt of the spirit world's presence. Fortunately, recordings still exist of these mesmerizing sittings on his website http://www.leslieflint.com. Whenever I listen to them, the hair on my arms stands up, as I can physically feel the invisible world speaking. The voices share epiphanies about being out of the body and talk about their observations of our world. We are so fortunate Leslie Flint had such passion to serve the spirit world. This ability has all but disappeared. I believe that's because it takes years of sitting with the spirit world for this ability to surface and refine.

Lastly, there is another trance medium I wish to mention named José Medrado. He has the remarkable ability to go into a deep trance and channel the souls of famous painters from the past like Renoir, Gauguin, Monet, Picasso, Toulouse-Lautrec, and Klimt by painting in the style of their art. In a deep trance and within five to ten minutes, he will produce a painting in the style of a master. His work is so authentic that his paintings are professionally recognized by museums. He uses his fingers as brushes. Stories have been shared that once living butterflies actually flew out of one of his paintings. The proceeds of his paintings go to an orphanage in Brazil. Fortunately, we are able to witness his work as there are YouTube videos celebrating his talent.

I describe these mediums to illustrate the amazing potential of combining with the spirit world. I believe we are really just touching what is possible. However, to progress, we must exercise discipline, trust, and patience to allow both worlds to work together. We must be open and spend time nurturing our connection to the spirit world.

The development of our ability to connect to spirit does not happen overnight nor should we become complacent with the level of mediumship as it presents today. My hope is that we keep expanding the questions and expectations of what is possible. If we perfect this art form, there could be great benefits for the world at large. Imagine if mediums with great integrity and talent were able, like Esther Hicks, to channel great minds from all time. Imagine spiritual TED talks where each participant had 20 minutes to bring forth wisdom from great minds in spirit. The speakers could be Jesus, Churchill, St. Joan of Arc, Lincoln, Queen Elizabeth I, or Gandhi. The spirit world is so deeply invested in our becoming. Imagine if we could consult the great minds of Einstein, Edison, Goethe, Michelangelo, and Da Vinci to comment upon the progress of the world or make suggestions. Beyond our personal need for healing and guidance, connecting to the spirit world is a conversation I feel we have barely begun to understand. I am grateful for institutions like the Arthur Findlay College in England for setting a standard of excellence in mediumship and exploring the spirit world.

DIVINE SPARK EXERCISES

136

- *Look at Your Beliefs:* We began the chapter talking about energy. Reflect upon these questions: Do you believe evil exists and why? What do you think a haunting is? Do souls get stuck? Have you experienced a soul imprint? What soul connection do you have to another that needs nurturing and love?

- *Soul Feeling:* Have a friend write down the first names of five people they know. Take the list and feel into each name. See if you can feel each name's personality, health, likes and dislikes, or sense a physical description based on how your body feels. You can also do this with people who are in the spirit world.

- *Soul Hearing:* Take a piece of music you love and try to follow one instrument through the song. Do this with each instrument you can perceive. Once finished, listen to the song again and appreciate all the work it took to create.

- *Learning from the Past:* Go to your ancestor tree within your soul seat. Call in an ancestor and ask them questions about their life: What are you most proud of? What was your first job? What were your hardships and regrets? What did you believe? Write down the information you receive and validate it with your family.

- *Pet Playtime:* Go to your ancestor tree and spend time with a pet you have loved in your life. I find the insight our pets have is miraculous. You can ask them what they were teaching you, what their gift was in your life, and what they want you to remember that you may forget about yourself.

- *Soul Sight:* Close your eyes and envision in your mind's eye a red apple. Observe the shape, size, and color. Do this for 20 seconds. Breathe in and exhale, releasing the apple. Envision in your mind's eye an orange. Witness its shape, size, and color. Look at the texture of its skin. Can you sense its smell or taste? Hold that image. Breathe in and exhale, releasing the orange. Now envision the apple and the orange next to each other. Can you hold each image strong with your soul sight? See how long you can keep both clear and vivid. Breathe in and release. Alter the exercise by using other objects and increase the number. See if you can work up to four apples, two oranges, and a banana, which looks like a spiritual smiley face with my soul sight.

- *Draw Your Ancestor Tree:* Write your experience connecting with your ancestor at your tree. Who showed up for you? Were they expected or unexpected? What did the shoes look like? What did your ancestor say to you? What wisdom did they offer?

Now that you have explored the places your soul can travel and who supports your soul, let's take some time to talk about nurturing your mind, body, and spirit.

PART THREE

SOUL-CENTERED LIVING

CHAPTER 8

Nurturing Your Soul

Whenever other worlds invite us, whenever we are balancing on the boundaries of our limited human condition, that's where life starts, that's where you start feeling yourself living.

—Phillippe Petit

Now that you have explored the landscape of your soul and connected to the spirit world, it is time to bring everything we have learned back to earth and integrate how to live a soul-centered life. This requires a shift in thinking. If our finite mind leads, we are a body and mind in search of our soul. When we are connected with our infinite self, we are a soul that has been gifted with a physical body and a mind through which to experience the natural world. This soul shift allows the infinite self to oversee and guide the finite self. We must honor both perspectives, because we cannot simply live spiritually, nor can we operate only from the finite self.

The yin and yang symbol illustrates that both the masculine and feminine natures within us complement each other in perfect harmony. To understand the duality of our own nature, we will spend the next two chapters exploring how inner balance will not only enhance your relationship with yourself but empower your relationships with others.

Although our physical body is either male or female, our soul essence has both masculine and feminine expressions. For instance, we can be nurturing, which is more feminine, yet dominant and aggressive when we are expressing our masculine energy. We must allow both nature's full expression.

To do this, let's look at how the masculine and feminine energies flow within your body. The right side of your brain controls the left side of your body. The energy of your soul within the left side of your body indicates how your feminine energy flows. Conversely, your left brain regulates the right side of the body which connects with the masculine expression of your soul. Let's begin by observing both natures within and around your physical body. Audio for the following practice is available at http://www.newharbinger.com /41849.

❋ EXERCISE ❋
Exploring the Duality Within Your Soul

141

Using your soul feeling, you will sense how your feminine and masculine energies play within your body. This is a great daily practice to help you become aware of just how different you are from day to day. This exercise can be done first thing when you wake up and right before you go to bed to help you witness how the events of your life impact your energy. You might want to draw a picture of your body and put your impressions on it after scanning each side.

Describing energy may seem challenging at first but can be fun once you get the hang of it. You may find words like bubbly, buzzy, dense, expanding, bouncy, or slippery give greater dimension to your perceptions. You can also feel temperature changes and if your soul vision is involved, you can see color as well. What you will discover exploring your soul will be completely unique to you, so the more you practice, the stronger your perceptions will become of the invisible world within and around you.

Bring your attention to the center of your mind and imagine you are floating right behind your eyes in the center of your head. Take a few minutes to just rest within this place. Become aware of the left side of your body. Begin by noticing the energy of your soul on that side. Focus on your left foot. Notice what parts of your foot you feel or don't feel. Is there tension? Does the energy move in a certain pattern? Just observe. Be curious. You may find certain places seem void of energy, which is perfectly normal. Focus on your entire left side, one part at a time, as you just did with your foot. Scan your ankle, shin, knee, thigh, hip, torso, arm, shoulder, neck, and head. Give each place time and your complete attention. Once you finish that scan, return to the center of your head. Take a deep breath in, exhale, and then open your eyes. Write down your answers to the following questions.

- What do you notice about the energy of the left side of your body?

- What energy words describe what you sensed?

- Where on the left side of your body do you currently experience physical pain or discomfort? What was it like to sense the energy of those locations?

- Do you have any joints on your left side that get cranky?

Repeat the above exercise, this time focusing on the right side of your body. Scan that side of your body from your right foot all the way up to the right side of your head, finishing by returning to the center of your mind as in the previous energy scan. Answer the above questions, this time reflecting your observations of the energy of your right side.

Now that you have observed both your feminine and masculine energy, what do you notice? Is there a difference between the energy of your right and left sides? Which side felt more active? Which side was more difficult to perceive?

With your new objective view of how the energy of your soul flows within you, let's explore the feminine and masculine natures and how their presence translates within us.

OUR DIVINE FEMININE

The left side of our bodies reflects your emotions and what we need and receive from the world. Using our chakra system as a grid, each chakra has masculine and feminine traits. Starting at the base chakra and working up to the crown, our feminine nature within each chakra desires comfort, pleasure, security, receiving love, connection, inner peace, and unity. Notice that each reflects qualities we can feel and receive from our environment and our relationships. When we are nurtured from the energy we receive and we communicate our emotions clearly, our left side will feel balanced. Our emotions are great indicators of how well we are allowing the feminine essence of our soul to flow within our body. If any of these qualities are not manifesting or are ignored, the energy of our soul will reflect the imbalance on our left side. Energy is never stuck; it just has different speeds and rhythms. Through energy awareness, we can nurture any perceived imbalances within our bodies. If our emotions are not expressed, we can become depressed, disconnected, confused, stuck, lethargic, needy, and detached from others and the world. If we are under-emotional, we will overthink and become resistant, cold, bitter, nervous, and uptight. When we are excessive or controlling of our emotions or do not communicate our needs fully, the left side of the body will often manifest pain or become energetically vulnerable, which makes those locations more susceptible to injury. Through your soul feeling, you can sense into the part of your body that is manifesting discomfort and ask yourself how it connects to your emotions and needs.

143

OUR DIVINE MASCULINE

The right side of the body mirrors how the masculine energy of our soul expresses itself in the world. Using the chakras as our guide, starting with the root, our masculine nature desires to survive, be satisfied, be powerful, express love, communicate, gain clarity, and connect to the universe. These needs are expressed outwardly into the world; therefore, balancing our masculine side requires we take action. How active and confident we are in achieving our wants and goals will be directly reflected in the flow of energy within our right side. When we do not act, the energy will remain within the body and create feelings of fear. If we continue not to act, we will feel hopeless, stagnant, stingy, diminished, and withdrawn. However, if we are too excessive with our active energy, we will be domineering, aggressive, controlling, manipulative, polarizing, forceful, and prideful. The goal is to maintain a power balance. How we feel and act contributes to our well-being and the health of all of our relationships, including the one we have with our self.

SEEING YOUR BODY AS A MAP

We are blessed to be able to improve our health by the choices we make. A balanced diet and exercise contribute greatly to the quality of our life. As a spiritual being, we must monitor how our energy moves and notice when we feel off or debilitated. Determining where our physical body has discomfort, pain, or injury can give us great insight into what lessons our soul is learning and where our resistance to those opportunities might be impacting our physical health.

The Energy of Your Feet

The first part of the body that begins your forward motion is your legs. They help you stand on the earth, stabilize your torso, and help you move. Your feet represent how you stand within the world. The left foot can indicate how connected you feel emotionally to the world and how comfortable you feel in your surroundings. The masculine energy flow of the right foot will indicate how confident you are in the actions you are taking and how willing you are to step forward and into your life. Some people lean forward and balance · more on their toes, while others sit back on their heels. Take a moment and notice how you stand. If you stand more on your toes, focus on being fully present within this moment. You may spend more time dreaming of or worrying about the future than focusing on what is currently within your life. Bring your weight back to center and breathe. You may sense your solar plexus a bit here, as being present may make you feel anxious. When your weight is too much on your heels, you can be a "pushover," which is what will happen if someone actually pushes you when your weight rests on the back of your feet. Work on noticing when you step back from your power or rely on others to take the lead. Within the arch point of each foot are smaller chakras. When you are feeling sick, exhausted, or are having issues breathing, envision opening up those chakras and pulling in the rich energy of the earth. I call this "breathing from your feet." It refreshes your legs and connects you to the earth. I do this when my energy gets low at the gym. Once I breathe from my feet, I find my energy replenishes and I can return to my workout.

145

The Energy of Your Knees

Before you physically step forward, you bend your leg at the knee. When you are fearful or emotionally resistant to truly stepping forward in your life, the first place that imbalance will manifest is in or around that joint. On the feminine side, your left knee will get your attention when you hold your emotions in instead of acknowledging or speaking your truth. This is heightened when you have to step into something new or own your power and stand up for yourself. If your right knee gives you issues, you may have communicated what you feel, and know what needs to change, yet remain fearful or hesitant about taking the necessary steps forward, just as I learned when I injured my own right knee (as mentioned in the passages about Soul Feeling in chapter 3).

The universe is very kind about change and will give us many indications, but if we do not acknowledge what needs to change, our lives will attract the necessary circumstances so our soul can continue to progress.

The Energy of Your Lower Torso

The pelvis and lower spine house the first and second chakras and are a storehouse for many issues in our childhood that relate to security and having our needs met. The left side of our body can also reflect our relationship with our mother and how we were nurtured, while the right side mirrors our relationship with our father. Within the pelvis are our sexual organs, so how comfortable we are expressing our sexuality will create flow or imbalance respectively. The following exercise will get you in touch with the energy of your lower back and pelvis. You can download audio for it at http://www .newharbinger.com/41849.

146

❋ EXERCISE ❋
Creating Flow in Your Lower Back and Pelvis

A simple and easy release for your pelvis and lower spine involves two yoga poses called the "cat" and "cow." Begin by kneeling with your hands on the floor and flatten your back like a table. Pull in your stomach towards your spine, arching your back toward the sky as you exhale out the mouth, bringing your chin gently toward your chest. Feel the stretch around your shoulders as well as in your lower back. Breathe a few breaths, deepening into cat pose. Release the pose and return to your flat back. In cow pose, imagine there is a string connecting your tailbone to the back of your head. Draw those two places gently together as your belly sinks toward the floor. Hold that pose for a full breath and then return to tabletop. Let's do the cat and cow pose together. Inhale and go into cow, pulling your head and tailbone toward each other, and exhale into cat pose with your spine arching toward the sky, finishing by returning to tabletop. This exercise is great for any lower back issues. As with any exercise, be gentle and never force your body into a pose. If there is discomfort, just breathe and expand into the limit of that pose.

The Energy of Your Chest

Within the chest are the lungs and the heart. Our lungs are the conduits through which we inhale and exhale the very life force that keeps us alive. When people are going through intense grief, I find their lungs will feel energetically heavy, almost as if breathing is a chore. In extreme cases, their chest will seem to cave in. Our breathing is very connected with our emotions. We will take in short breaths when we're excited, nervous, and scared. Some people have deeper inhales and shorter exhales. Take a moment and witness your breathing. Which is shorter or longer? Are you a shallow breather? Our ability to take in oxygen assists our body in so many ways. If you have issues with your left lung, ask yourself what grief you may be holding onto or where you may feel hesitant about receiving. I find the left lung relates to inhaling life. Conversely, the right lung is about moving forward with grief and letting go deeply of what has been lost or loved.

Our heart is an emotional center, so the chest area clearly reflects our feelings and how willing we are to process them. When I sit with a person who has experienced a breakup of a relationship, the energy of their heart will almost seem to pull inward. I will see an empty space within their chest as if the lost love has created an energetic hole. It is a great practice to keep tabs on your ability to give and receive love, as those flows are best when they are balanced. Not only must we feel love, we must be willing to express it. If our emotions remain contained within, we can become resentful that others do not know what we need. It all begins with us and how willing we are to teach other people how to treat us. This is especially true for people who have issues with their heart. Our heart keeps the flow of our blood coursing through our body, so minding our emotional flow complements that organ function. You can find audio for the following chest energy practice at http://www.newharbinger.com/41849.

✸ EXERCISE ✸
Creating Flow in Your Chest

The "cobra" yoga pose is a great heart opener. Lie stomach down on the ground with your palms pressed evenly against the floor just below your shoulders. Slowly press into the floor, lifting your chest toward the sky. Keep your core engaged, your hip bones and the tops of your feet on the floor while you gaze upward. Breathe and hold this pose for a few breaths, then gently ease yourself back to the floor, resting your head on one cheek. Repeat this exercise a few times. Progressively work to lift your torso more and more off the floor till your arms are straightened. Just remember to breathe and always focus on relaxing into each pose.

The Energy of Your Upper Back

The upper back, especially the rhomboids, or the muscles that connect the scapula to the vertebrae, are a storage house for anger, rage and resentment. This area is the backside of your heart. If you find your upper back on the left side is tense, assess your anger, rage, and resentment levels. Ask yourself what you are angry about. Honor these powerful feelings. If your right side is grumpy, you may need to take some action steps toward changing what is causing those emotions to be held in your body. Begin by asking yourself where you are resisting receiving or giving love. Near the winter holidays, so many of my clients have issues with that part of their back. Nothing brings up our spiritual homework like spending time with our families during the holidays. Should this area get tense for you, the cobra and cat-cow poses will help. Or it just might be time for a massage.

The shoulders hold the energy of our responsibilities. We can carry the weight of the world on our shoulders. Look at your shoulders in the mirror; you may observe if one is higher than the other. If your left side is higher, you may be holding onto emotions of resentment or frustration, or simply be overwhelmed by your current responsibilities. Are you allowing yourself to process those feelings? Do you need to say "no" to someone to lighten your load? If your right shoulder is higher or more stressed, what responsibilities are you holding that could be reduced or delegated? What action steps can you take to lighten your load? Due to our use of computers and phones, most of our shoulders curve forward, because we are always looking down. Shoulders that are more concave can indicate you are protecting your heart. It is challenging to be vulnerable, but practicing rolling your shoulders back, with a focus on pulling the rhomboids together, opens up the heart. When the shoulders are pulled back too much, this can indicate a tightening of the back muscles, especially the rhomboids. When we maintain our feelings of anger and frustration over time, we can cause the fascia, or the protective sheath that covers our muscles, to tighten, resulting in a permanent altering of our frame. Our emotions are meant to be felt, expressed, and released. Otherwise, we will store their energy within and create tight, tense muscles. The cat and cow yoga poses help this region as well.

149

The Energy of Your Arms

Your arms extend from your chest and carry the energy of your heart. They allow you to express your love and animate your soul. Through your arms and hands, your soul articulates itself by caressing, holding, creating, building, writing, gesturing, and loving. Energy practitioners channel their heart energy though their arms when they are open to being of service. If your left arm is debilitated, check in to your heart and see where you are resisting receiving love or touch. If your right arm draws your attention, reflect on how you can express your love through touch, action, or deed.

The Energy of Your Neck

Our neck is a fascinating location for our soul's energy. I find issues arise here when there is a disconnection between how we feel and what we think. I get migraines. They manifest in my neck prior to arriving in my head. I use my mind and nervous system quite profoundly in my work of being open to the spirit world, so my neck will always help me know when I need to take a break. If your neck has issues on your left side, see if your thoughts and emotions can be articulated in a nurturing and supportive manner. Consider if you are overthinking what is happening in your life or if you are disconnecting to how you feel. If the right side of your neck is problematic, reflect on what you must do to activate positive change, so your feelings and actions are equally honored. You may be overthinking your action step, or feeling fear about initiating the change. I also find my neck gives me trouble when I am getting signs I need to do something, but my mind seems to disagree. You can access audio for the neck energy practice below at http://www.newharbinger.com/41849.

❋ EXERCISE ❋
Creating Flow in Your Neck

Stretch your neck forward so your chin falls toward the chest, relaxing the back of your neck. Gently push down your shoulders and press your rhomboids together. Slowly lift your chin toward the sky, jutting out your lower jaw to stretch the front of the neck. To stretch the sides of your neck, gently draw your left ear toward your left shoulder, feeling the stretch on the right side of your neck and pushing your right shoulder down. Hold for a few breaths. Then repeat the same with your right ear reaching toward your right shoulder, stretching the left side of your neck, keeping your left shoulder down. Check to make sure your shoulders stay relaxed and do not lift up.

The Energy of Your Face

The jaw allows your mouth to open and your feelings and voice to be heard. Our jaws hold the tension of what is unsaid, along with our frustrations and deep sadness. Those that clench their jaws or grind their teeth often need to give themselves permission to express how they feel. Such expression can be especially helpful for people who were disallowed that freedom in their childhoods. Should your jaw be tense, massage the mandibular joint at the back of the jaw under your ears; however, go lightly, as it is a very tender area. Yawning helps release that joint as well. However, you are apt to start a yawning epidemic around you.

The Energy of Your Eyes

Your eyes represent your ability to see what is going on. If your left eye is compromised, there may be resistance to seeing a situation or personal experience clearly because of overwhelming emotions. If your right eye has issues, allow yourself to envision what you wish to change and take the necessary steps to acknowledge and honor what needs to be released. If you are unclear what the next step might be, try focusing on an outcome that would best honor all involved. This also helps those realities manifest.

151

The Energy of Your Ears

Your ears take in what others say to you and connect you to the environment around you. When we are around someone we have challenges with, our ears can stop hearing. I have known clients whose left or emotionally sensitive ear will almost go deaf, so they do not have to listen to what others are saying or feeling. Conversely, if the right ear is challenged, ask yourself what you need to do that perhaps you have received advice about or know is the right course of action. This is also a sensitive area for those of us who have strong soul hearing. As my work has progressed, I have less and less tolerance for loud noise. I always have earplugs with me to honor my ears. It can be a loud world sometimes, so take care of these amazing instruments.

The Energy of Your Nose

Our nose takes in our breath, so when there are nose issues, like snoring, we may be resistant to what is new. Certainly, there are physical reasons for snoring, but it is valid to explore all options, both physical and spiritual. I also find people snore if their needs are not being met. The use of a neti pot for nasal irrigation is great for clearing congestion and opening up the sinuses.

We are fortunate to have many mind/body practitioners who recognize the deep correlation between our bodies and our finite self. Somatic healing, neurolinguistic reprogramming, and tapping are just a few of the options you can explore to help align your overall health.

My hope for offering a physical map of where your body can hold different emotions and tensions is to empower you to recognize how much your body reflects your finite self. There are times that a situation creates an injury, but the location of the injury can equally reflect when we are out of alignment with our soul. Noticing how the energy flows within your body can help you create physical and spiritual balance.

EMBRACING YOUR POWER

Shape-shifting is a way for your soul to feel power that you might not otherwise own. Animals never doubt their power, so blending with spirit animals is a great way to explore your masculine and feminine energies. The following is a meditation to help you align, identify, and step into your divine feminine essence. Visit http://www.newharbinger.com/41849 to download audio for this meditation.

❋ EXERCISE ❋
Embracing Your Feminine Power Animal

Imagine you are standing at the edge of a forest. Before you is a path. It is inviting and your curiosity compels you to follow it. You hear the crunch of the leaves below your feet and witness the canopy of trees above. You feel safe and nurtured. You are drawn to the center of the forest and find a clearing. It is a near-perfect circle surrounded by tall trees. You walk to the center of this sacred open space. You know you have come here for a reason. You become aware of movement in the forest and amongst the trees surrounding you. You do not feel afraid. You are being stalked by a powerful female animal. Feel her energy moving all around you and all at once she enters the circle. Take in her focused, loving, fearless, and deep soul. She is stunning and powerful. She is your fully expressed divine feminine nature. Watch as she circles around you. She represents all of your grace, darkness, nurturing, and emotional depth. She is maternal and fiercely loves and protects you. Witness how she walks on the earth. Catch her gaze. Look deeply within her eyes and in that moment you become her. You are her and she is you. Blend into the fullness of her physical body. Feel her muscles and the architecture of her body. Feel her power of intuition, knowing without judging. Feel the dynamic depth of her love, clarity, and strength. As you enter the forest, night falls. It is deep darkest night and quiet. Yet, without sight, you see everything. You charge full speed through the forest, feeling your heart guiding your direction. Witness the purity of focus and determination. You move with ease and grace. You arrive. Discover your children. These little souls you have birthed through your body one by one. Feel the ability to give birth and create. Feel the depth of your unconditional love, dedication, and dynamic fierceness to protect them. Look into the eyes of your children and see what they can see within you. Can you feel their trust, playfulness, and purity?

153

In a moment, you are back within the forest, moving full speed into a cave. You enter without fear and look within the darkness of your soul. What do you see? What is changing within you? What do you need to acknowledge that must be released? What is in the shadows of your life waiting to be brought into the light? Back out in the forest, you return to the circle and back to the grove of trees. Step out of her and become you. Thank her soul and watch as she disappears again into the forest. Find your way back to the path and to the beginning of the forest. When you are ready, open your eyes.

Take a moment to write down any observations that you noticed. How did it feel to explore the wild untamed feminine nature? What did you learn about her trust in darkness? How did it feel to witness your children and feel their love? What did you see within the cave? What does her soul make you realize about how you connect to the fullness of your divine feminine?

Now, let's get in touch with the energy of the divine masculine by meeting a power animal that represents it. You can find audio for the following meditation at http://www.newharbinger.com/41849.

❀ EXERCISE ❀
Embracing Your Masculine Power Animal

Daylight reveals the forest path and again you are drawn to the sacred open space surrounded by trees. You are aware of being watched, perhaps from around or above. You feel an approaching animal's power, instinct, and authority. Witness as your divine masculine animal enters the circle. Watch him move as he comes close. Observe his focused gaze on you, eyes locked in intensity. Look into his eyes deeply and see into his soul. As you do, you become him and he becomes you. Expand your awareness to fill all of his body. Feel your connection to the earth, yet your full awareness of what is around you. Feel your powerful physical form, clear mind, and loyal heart. You lead by example and with authority steeped in love. Feel it within your body. In a second, your form charges at full speed into the hot sunlit forest, sensing all that is around you. You know no fear. Every creature watches you with respect, as you honor their presence and hold your power with integrity. You are pure motion and intention. You run at full speed to a cliff. As you stop, you take in the vista below you. Look into the landscape of your future potential. Everything is possible. What do you see? What desires are visible? What potential destinies are laid out before you? All are yours to have and explore. You feel the sun's warmth streaming down and in that moment, you breathe in the light. As your power expands, so does your physical presence. You become larger and larger until you are bigger than all around you. You sit on this cliff knowing anything is yours for the taking. No challenges, just unlimited opportunities to devour and conquer. You make a sound that echoes into all the places and spaces you see. Hear how the world goes quiet awaiting your next move. You are power and light. Pure possibility. Within a moment, back to regular size, you find yourself back in the circle. You step out of your masculine animal and gaze with gratitude into his eyes. As you thank your friend, he becomes pure light and vanishes into thin air. Find your way out of the sacred circle, back to the path, back to the beginning, standing on the edge of the forest. When you are ready, open your eyes.

155

✳

Take a moment and reflect upon the following questions: When you became the masculine animal, how did it feel? How was it different from the feminine animal? How did it feel to be fearless? Where did you feel that within your body? What did he teach you? What did you see looking out at the landscape of your soul? What destinies and potential futures did you witness? How did it feel to know you are pure potential and the universe awaits your every step?

Working with animals is a great way to discover the freedom you can have when your fear is not present. Animals are instinctual, so they are not distracted by the doubts, fears, or insecurity of our finite self. I have had great journeys with animals and have realized their guidance can be dynamic. Shape-shifting, or the ability to become something other than ourselves, is a great soul tool. By blending with another soul, our compassion and empathy allows us to understand ourselves in different and dynamic ways. You can always return to the clearing in the forest and revisit these new friends.

When you are feeling disempowered, practice blending with either your masculine or feminine animal guide. I have long worked with a jaguar guide. When I first met her, I was scared, because I had not owned my strength and ferocity. She has proven to be a great indicator of how balanced my emotions are. If I call her in and she looks sad or injured, I know to look within my soul at what I am ignoring within myself. If I have an event and I call her to my side, she will often appear as big as the room, so I know she is asking me to own my own space and get ready for a great experience. Just like any relationship, these ones must be nurtured. Go online and research the animals that revealed themselves to you. Each animal has *medicine*, or spiritual gifts that they offer. You can get a talisman for each and put it in some sacred place within your home. The point is to honor and respect your animal guides' invitation to teach you. Lastly, they have a great sense of humor. When I am teaching, I find people have an easier time working with animals and see just how human their love can be. They can tease us, because we certainly take this thing called life a little too seriously and they will be the first ones to remind us this is so.

RECHARGING YOUR SOUL

Sometimes you just need a little recharge and love. There are a number of ways you can nurture the energy of your soul within your body. Although most energy treatments are subtle, depending on your sensitivity, they can be rather powerful as well. One of the most established traditions is Chinese medicine. Whenever I have something occur in my body that indicates imbalance, my first exploration is always acupuncture. Practitioners begin by feeling the different pulses on your wrist or looking at your tongue to determine how the energy flows through your body. Small needles are inserted along energy pathways or meridians within the body that correspond to different organs and master energy flows. Depending on how sensitive you are, you can feel the movement of *qi* or *chi*, the vital life force energy within you, as it realigns and flows, allowing your body's natural healing response to commence. Each meridian connects to the others, so it is like a grand baton race of light occurring within your body. After the needles or other modalities have been administered, you are gifted with at least 20 minutes of quiet or naptime like when you were a kid. I finish treatments feeling refreshed, renewed, and reenergized.

Tai chi and qigong are two great ways to work your physical and energetic bodies at the same time. Each method honors the meridians of the body and helps your *qi* flow though subtle exercises and poses. You could look at both of these as movement meditations, as you are focusing your attention on your breath while moving your body. Qigong is widely practiced in China and often prescribed as a healing modality after surgery. Your body can also benefit from movement practices like yoga and pilates. Yoga does so much good for our soul and I am thrilled at all the different forms and practices, as well as its popularity. Pilates works wonders to align your body through stretching and challenging poses.

157

As far as energy healing practitioners, there are many different hands-on healing techniques. These range from acupressure and subtle touch to craniosacral therapy, emotional freedom techniques (EFT), quantum touch, and reiki. I have explored water treatments like *watsu*, which is like dancing and rebirth all at once. I studied *jin shin jyutsu*, a Japanese hands-on healing technique that combines the acupuncture meridians with a rich spiritual integration. In that practice, I saw light within my body for the first time. My suggestion is to research and learn. Discover what makes you most comfortable.

Barbara Brennan and Donna Eden have respectively created integral and intelligent energy medicine schools that produce very well-trained certified practitioners who work above the body or with a light touch. Empower yourself to research your practitioner. They should never be defensive if you ask about their training or years in practice. Such information should be readily available on their website. I am a huge fan of study, so honor your soul by choosing the right practitioner.

Finally, the most powerful energy healing transformations I have witnessed have transpired within my shamanic practice. Shamanic practitioners facilitate profound soul work which can shift how you frame the experiences of your life. They can help you connect to your personal power, honor your life transitions, shift the energy of what no longer serves you, and connect you to Mother Earth. Although many people currently call themselves shamans, the only true shamans are the indigenous people. What we practice is modern shamanism or an adaptation of what their relationship with the earth taught them. It is an oral tradition passed own from mentor to student. My training took over four years. Before I was ready to work with others, I needed to walk the medicine wheel personally to understand the power of indigenous medicine and to deeply untangle the depths of my soul. Practitioners need to be working on their own challenges. Shamanic work is very deep and intense, but it also produces magical shifts. Should you wish to work with a shaman, please research their background. The Four Winds, a shamanic training organization created by Alberto Villoldo, deeply trains their practitioners. Modern shamans can work remotely, but sometimes you may wish to work in person. Their site, https://www.thefourwinds.com, lists practitioners by state, so you can find someone within your area. No matter what modality draws you, energy medicine is soul nurturing. Research and discover what feeds your soul.

Energy practitioners are both intuitives and visionaries of your soul. The tricky moniker is "healer." We do not heal—that part is all you. You must be willing to receive and release all that connects to why your energy is not flowing as it should. Our job is to sense the movement of energy within your soul. The best energy practitioners I know can see your energy. The practitioner's responsibility is to create a sacred environment for the highest good to be made available for your soul. Energy work requires immense integrity because we are working on the level of the soul. The intent of the practitioner should always be to empower you to heal, not make you reliant upon what they do for you. If their ego is too evident, then see that as a red flag. Their job is to create the best possible environment for you to let go what no longer serves you and to draw to you your highest potential.

As human beings, we are meant be in motion. Whether you swim, bike, hike, walk, climb, stretch, do down dog, kick, do hundreds, punch, or spin, keep the sacred vehicle of your soul nurtured by staying active and moving. We are energy first, so movement is a must.

159

CHAPTER 9

Cultivating Soul-Centered Relationships

The meeting of two personalities is like the contact of two chemical substances: if there is any reaction, both are transformed.

—Carl Jung

"Your father is joining us," I said to my client, as the room became noticeably cool. As I blended with her dad's soul, I felt immediately sarcastic and thirsty for anything alcoholic. He guided me back in time to the family living room where my client had grown up. He and I stood side by side. I followed his glance to a chair that lifted into the air in slow motion, then crashed down hard, smashing on the floor and sending shards in all directions. Each object he focused on seemed to spontaneously combust, until the entire room looked as if it had been hit by a tornado. I witnessed my client's mom try to intervene and stop the destruction. As everything went momentarily dark, I was overwhelmed with the sounds of flesh slaps. A few moments later, lights up, a crash on the floor, and he was down for the count. Their living room was a battlefield where alcohol triumphed until the beast passed out.

With his left cheek pressed into the grooves of the wooden floor, the father's soul guided me to focus on his feet. Mud was still embedded in the rims and soles of his shoes from his daily labor. I witnessed shaking little five-year-old hands carefully tying each shoe's laces in perfect bows. I came back into my office fully aware, as my client said in bewilderment, "No one knew I did that. I was afraid he would wake up, but I did not want him to stand up and trip because his laces were undone."

As my client finished speaking, I witnessed her father's soul taking in this innocent act of love as if for the first time. His daughter's words infused his soul like a gentle breeze and he softened and expanded fully into his soul space. As the emotions collected in his throat, he said to me, "Thank her for that and for inviting me."

I repeated this to her and she stared at me, transfixed. "I did invite him, in the car on the way over to your office. I told him, 'I have no idea what you could say to me and I really don't care. If you have something to say then just say it and leave, but either way, I really don't care.' I never asked to speak to him before because I never thought it would make a difference. Then he showed you his shoes, the most nonthreatening symbol that would validate his presence. The shoes changed *everything* for me. Half of my rage with him was because I never thought he would truly understand the havoc he wreaked or the impact of his actions. The shoes changed everything when you mentioned them. He saw what I did. We all tried to help him. I can finally work toward forgiveness. I have been waiting my whole life for this."

This daughter gave her spirit dad a huge gift by allowing his soul an opportunity to be accountable. Notice that she invited him without expectation. Had she dismissed him or his soul not chosen to partake in this opportunity, neither would have evolved. It was her openness and hope for a soul conversation that changed everything.

The human goal of mediumship is to prove the immortailty of our soul past the change called death. However, the spirit world's intention for soul conversations will always be healing. Our departed loved ones witness the residue of their unfinished business and just how much it affects our ability to live freely and fully. They see mediumship as an opportunity to touch once again into this realm and attempt to shift the stories we maintain that limit us. Their hope is to progress their souls and ours by being accountable. This is why, if you go to a medium, it is important to have no expectations about who comes forward. Our finite self loves to try to control what it does not understand. You may wish a pleasant reunion with your favorite aunt, but instead find your grandfather who terrified your father will come through instead. I know their presence is an incredible spiritunity. Coming from our finite self, our resentment and fear will demand these souls be dismissed, but the infinite self sees the encounter as a means to understand and reframe the stories of our past. In doing so, we can release the history of our pain in order to update our relationships with the souls in the spirit world.

By claiming complete ownership of all you feel, think, say, and do, you will contribute and expand this world and not leave any unfinished business that others within your soul circle or environment need to progress for you.

162

OUR LOVE OF DRAMA

To have soul-centered relationships requires mindfulness, self-reflection, and patience. We have to be willing to observe *how* we relate to others, as well as ask ourselves *why* we respond that way.

Because we have natural and human-inspired disasters, there are individuals whose job requires they risk their life for others to keep the peace, and maintain balance in our society. In those circumstances, we have real victims, rescuers, and persecutors. Those roles become disempowering when we play victim, rescuer, and persecutor within our own relationships to avoid conflict and potential evolution. This was the great realization of Stephen Karpman in 1968 when he introduced the drama triangle. The drama triangle highlights why our relationships become disempowered when we assume one of three roles: rescuer, victim, or persecutor.

Understanding the roles of the triangle has allowed me and now my clients to witness the imbalance we create when we overstep our bounds, give up, or dominate and criticize others. Each of us defaults to one role most naturally. No matter how we participate, we will always end up as the victim. I will refer to the drama triangle going further as the FST or "finite self triangle," because we engage in drama solely with the finite self. When we are guided by our emotions and ego alone, without the wisdom of the soul, there will always be drama. Let's look at each role more deeply.

Finite Self Triangle
FST

Persecutor
"I dominate"

Rescuer
"I fix"

Victim
"I can't"

163

Rescuers

Most of the people who will be drawn to this book will naturally step into the FST in the role of rescuer. Rescuers are inherently good people, because we truly wish to help others and the world. Our main need is validation and acceptance, because we operate under the myth that we are not good enough. In order to play this role, we need someone who needs our help, so we naturally attract people who play the victim. Their problem becomes our problem and in that moment, we know who we are and what to do. Nurturing is healthy, but where we often go off track is when we try to "fix" someone or something. I know this because I am a recovering rescuer. Where I gained great insight was when I looked into why I wanted to fix other people's issues. My conclusion disturbed me greatly, because I was under the illusion that I was helping someone.

What I discovered was I tried to rescue because I did not want to feel the helplessness and powerlessness that the victim felt, because I knew those feelings all too well. I was rescuing to avoid the feeling of being disempowered. Rescuers also help others so we do not have to look at what needs to be loved and addressed within our own self.

Rescuers can come from families where one parent was unstable or unreliable. We emerge from these families with a highly acute sense of soul feeling. This is developed early because we are always checking into the energy of the environment around us to make sure we or those we "protect" are safe. If we sense the unstable person is okay, then we are okay. If they are off balance, we must prepare for the unknown. Fear becomes something we expect to encounter. Therefore "Are you okay, because if you are okay, then I am okay" becomes the mental pattern we default to in our future relationships. We learn that if we do more for others, they will like us and we will feel needed and safe. Because we are always monitoring the energy outside of our own soul space, rescuers tether to another person's aura to create a feeling of connection. We sense others through the third chakra. This is why so many nurturers have sensitive stomachs, because we overtax the energy that emits from our solar plexus. This improperly balanced energy exchange is the quintessential reason for the codependent relationships we can attract.

Rescuers often stay in relationships long after they are over. They may not wish to hurt the feelings of their partner or wait for a better time. This supports the pattern where the other person becomes more important than the rescuer is. They will think they are being considerate by taking care of the other person. In this way, nurturers do not create balanced relationships playing this role, because they are always helping the other while delaying their own evolution.

Please note that if you experience any emotions, tightness within your third chakra or thoat, or have sudden desire to stop reading, you may be deeply connecting to the role of rescuer. We strive to be the good child, the people pleaser, but often neglect our own discontent. We can become resentful, exhausted, and unhealthy, because we do not prioritize our own needs being met. We will give until we have to stop. We crave acknowledgment because we do not know we are valuable. We often rescue without an invitation. When the person we have started helping without permission becomes angry with us, we feel unappreciated, invisible, unloved, and not enough. It is at that point we shift from rescuer to victim.

Victims

People who assume the victim role do not have strong confidence in themselves or their abilities. They are unable to help themselves because they feel defective somehow. They can be the problem child, the sick one, or the black sheep of the family. From their perspective, the situation or position they are in seems unfixable, so they feel powerless and hopeless to make changes. This is catnip to the rescuer. People who take on the victim role believe life happens *to* them, not *for* them, so they rarely take responsibility for their actions. Others are to blame: their parents, their health, mercury in retrograde, anything that exonerates them. They can be sensitive, moody, and avoid eye contact. Victims do not feel their opinion matters. They are always comparing themselves to others' success, work ethic, or fortune. Since their mantra is "I can't," they can avoid taking initiative, solving issues, or making decisions. They assume it just won't work, so they don't even try. When they complain, there is always someone to listen who will help fix their predicament, so they never have to take action. The energy expression of a victim is a pulling in or hooking into the energy field of others, like they are casting a fishing line. Victims create a tight, almost claustrophobic energy loop between themselves and their savior. Where this loop becomes dysfunctional is when the rescuer seeks approval and validation. If the victim has to give that appreciation to another, the very thing they are needing themselves, it only reminds them of their own inadequacies. Therefore, the victim eventually becomes resentful and bitter to those who help them, because the ability of others to find solutions validates their belief that they are hopeless. Since the victim also knows secretly that they are capable, their resentment can often shift them to the persecutor role, and once again, the rescuer becomes the victim. The finite self of the victim will always focus upon what is not working. The people around them may become exhausted by their discontent and inability to take action, therefore isolating the victim further.

Persecutors

Persecutors are the most difficult role for us to acknowledge we play. Yet, we all become controlling, rigid, impatient, and criticizing to others because we feel we have a better idea or could do something more efficiently. We finger point, accuse, and intimidate. Our social media habits allow us to rant against others, a different kind of human pollution, without discernment, apology, or ownership of how those opinions affect others. We blame the government, the environment, other countries, and individuals for injustices and rules that we are averse to. These days, we step into this role more frequently and publicly.

I have found people who step into the FST as persecutors do not feel they are loveable. Many experienced some kind of abuse or abandonment in their early life. Their energetic memory of love is disconnection, so they expect and create this within their own relationships. Imagine there is a line of energy between a parent and a child. That line between them drops or disconnects when the parent's behavior is overly aggressive or when they are absent. The persecutor will seek out that energy pattern in their relationships, so they will expect abandonment. This explains why they may have issues trusting people or why they do not expect people to stay. Sadly, because that is their expectation, they create that reality in their life in two different ways. In one scenario, the persecutor will rely on and smother a partner to the point that the partner feels suffocated and leaves. The other way is the persecutor will attract a partner, become really close, and just when the persecutor experiences vulnerability or love, they will terminate the relationship suddenly to maintain control. In both scenarios they create outcomes that mirror their belief that love means disconnection so everyone leaves.

Much like many animals expand their physical presence to become as large as they can to intimidate others, persecutors will expand their energy out to dominate others. They do this by being self-righteous, disrespecting personal space, blaming, shaming, and criticizing. They put themselves above others by always being right, needing to win, dominating, and demanding others meet their standards. They highlight others' limitations. They can be aloof and difficult to love, because their actions and words protect their vulnerability. You will rarely want to feel connected to them emotionally, because it just does not feel safe. Through domination and inaccessibility, the persecutors achieve and again create the reality that everyone leaves them.

Rescuers attract the victims who need help, but for a victim to believe they are powerless, they equally attract persecutors. Since persecutors erroneously feel they are unworthy of love or unlovable, they attract rescuers. Each role teaches us that our beliefs truly create our experience. As long as we are playing any of these FST roles, we can never feel secure, loved, or enough. There will always be drama.

Now that we have examined the three FST roles, let me give you a personal example to help illustrate how easily we can play all the roles. This was not a proud moment of mine, but this experience proved invaluable to me. It helped me realize I needed to adjust my behavior and work on why I was always trying to fix and rescue.

I was working at a job I loved. Two strong and capable ladies I had the fortune of working with complained about a man in our organization who was mistreating them. I was included in their conversations, and over time, I just got more and more angry. They chose to do nothing, which fueled my anger even more. One day, I decided something had to be done. Without their permission, I went to the person they were complaining about and told him everything, all with the intention of being a good friend and helping everyone. The man I approached understandably was defensive and denied their accusations. When the ladies found out I had said something, they became incredibly angry with me, as well as feared they would lose their jobs. Not surprisingly, I lost all of their friendships and eventually quit my job because I had created tremendous tension and drama.

Let me break down how each of us played every role in that scenario. First of all, I stepped in as rescuer. I did not have these ladies' permission, nor was this my problem. The real reason I became mad was because a similar thing had happened to me in the past and I never stood up for myself. My anger was my own, not theirs. I stepped into the persecutor role when I approached the man the ladies had issue with. Since he denied the accusation, I became mad at him. He became the momentary victim. When the ladies found out I talked to him without their permission, they got mad at me, so they shifted to persecutor and victim when they feared they could lose their jobs. I landed in victim because everyone was mad at me for stepping into something that was truly none of my business. I became labeled as a troublemaker at work, which, for a rescuer who tried to be the good girl, was devastating to me. At the time, I felt that I had done everything right. I could not understand why everyone was so mad at me, which made me feel isolated and misunderstood. Finally, I took no responsibility for my participation in the event. I made myself a perfect victim. Thank god I understand it all now. I forgive myself for not knowing better and hope they all do in time. I created a huge amount of drama all because I thought I could fix the situation for everyone.

This pattern has clearly been a great soul lesson for me. The main roles I play are rescuer and victim. I have attracted many situations that helped me realize this. What saved me was my soul. From the infinite self, I could step out of the FST, witness what was going on, and love myself for the mess I created.

We will always be tested after we have transcended a lesson to allow us to revisit our new instincts. Last summer, my wallet was stolen and I immediately felt a descent into victim. But, this time, I realized I had a choice to navigate my emotions with the discernment of my soul. I had a good soul conversation with myself about the fear and victimization I was feeling. I had a few moments where I was overwhelmed, but I simply focused on nurturing my feelings of fear as they arose. The spiritunity for me was to reframe what happened. I was not a victim, but rather I was participating in a greater play where my soul was a minor character in someone else's drama. By viewing the situation from the idea that life happens for me instead of to me, I was able to shift my feelings of disempowerment to empowerment within three hours after the incident. I even prayed that the person who stole my wallet benefited from what they obtained and that miracles happened for them.

We will attract what we need to grow until we learn the lesson. That is why we experience similar situations over and over again. We are not stuck, just learning.

We cannot control what happens to us, but we can control how we respond. So let's look at the roles we play and how we can truly empower our relationships by stepping out of the FST.

SOUL-CENTERED RELATIONSHIPS

Each of the FST roles has a soul-centered counterpart. Let's look at how the victim, rescuer, and persecutor can be nurtured by our soul.

The Soul-Centered Child

Victims feel helpless. They look to others to help, because they are convinced they are unable to do things by themselves. They can feel their needs are not met. When we step into the role of victim, it is our "little you" or soul-centered child who can help. When we are connected to our soul-centered child, we are playful, creative, and open. Children learn by trial and error. They do not know how to walk, but they keep trying until they do. We can't walk for them; it is their job to discover they can. We will always need support from others. But by learning to take baby steps and remembering we are much stronger than we think, we can find joy and excitement in what we do not know. When you go to the victim role, think of that part of you as a child who needs your love, support, and encouragement. When you default to victim, also see if your soul-centered nurturing may provide necessary comfort.

The Soul-Centered Nurturer

When we rescue, our intention may be sincere, but our approach is off. The desire of the rescuer is to connect, however, since we do not have a strong sense of self-worth, we often overcompensate. Equally, we may step into that role because we do not want to feel the helplessness of the victim. What we need is support and love. Our divine feminine or the yin aspect of our soul nurtures the rescuer. When the balanced feminine nature of our soul expresses itself, we are love personified. We are passive and receptive, which may seem contrary, but being available and open is exactly what is needed. We do not jump in without invitation, but rather witness the other soul and allow their own personal discovery as a necessary part of their evolution. Part of the feminine aspect within all of us is introspective. That quality is exactly what we may need to unearth why we are rescuing in the first place. Through loving self-examination, we can begin to seek the origins of our lack of self-worth. Once we nurture our own finite self, we can then apply our intuition and spontaneity to be of service to others. When we truly surrender to being of service, we are void of agenda and can simply focus all of our loving tenderness on the soul we are supporting. Our divine feminine can help us nurture what emotionally comes up for us when we feel another person's vulnerability. By honoring our own needs first and making sure we are okay, we can truly be of service to others.

Most people who are drawn to caregiving professions must learn deep self-care, because many will give until their health is compromised. By creating proper boundaries and limits to when and how much we give, we can then hold a sacred space for others and allow them to discover their own soul lessons without any adverse emotions arising within us. In doing so, we empower them not by fixing and denying them crucial experiences, but by witnessing their process and trusting that what happens is perfect for their evolution. This avails us to explore the creative power of our own divine feminine nature fully so we can evolve our own soul.

Soul Centered Star
SCS
Soul-Centered Child

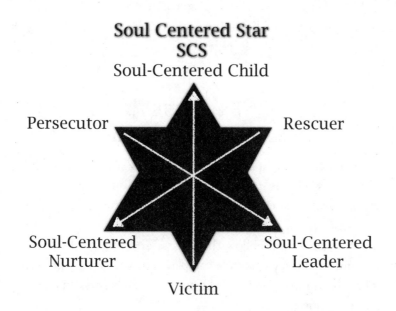

Persecutor

Rescuer

Soul-Centered
Nurturer

Soul-Centered
Leader

Victim

The Soul-Centered Leader

Finally, the balanced divine masculine empowers the persecutor. When we are connected to our masculine nature we are powerful. We possess two great attributes of a leader: discipline and action. When we express our masculine nature healthfully, we act, initiate, activate, plan, focus, and inspire others by showing what is possible within themselves. We actively engage and analyze what comes our way. We generate a focused and logical approach to the forward motion in our lives. Although this can be an independent motivation, we are always aware that no one is greater than or less than: we are all equal. We are all connected. As we overcome and triumph over our own adversities, we inspire others to discover that tenacity and perseverance within themselves. There is not a personal gain, but a collective expansion into the right course of action for all.

When our divine masculine leads, we step into our own empowerment and allow others to equally activate their authentic assertiveness, without dominating or diminishing others. This logical, rational, and extroverted aspect balances our more empathic, intuitive, and introverted feminine self. By knowing the soul-centered equivalents to the FST roles, you can work toward evolving the drama in your life.

✸ EXERCISE ✸
Soul-Centered Insight

Soul-centered insight comes from balancing your finite and infinite selves. This is important because in disagreements where we default to the ego and emotions of the finite self, we often energetically disconnect from the very people who are teaching us about ourselves. Follow these steps and you will be able to nurture and notice what role you play, why you engage, and how it has shaped who you are. Take out your journal and answer the following questions.

- Which role do I play most often?

- How does that role make me feel emotionally?

- Where do I feel that within my body?

- What memory comes up around this feeling?

- Freeze frame the memory and cast all the participants in the correct FST roles.

- List three words that describe the authority figure involved.

- List three words that describe you at the time.

- If the authority figure was a child standing before you, what would they need to hear from your divine feminine? These responses should be loving and tender.

- Write a positive affirmation about who you have become from this situation, starting with "I am." Example: I am self-reliant and dependable. I am visible and loveable. Dig deep.

✸

The only way to diminish the drama is to not participate in the FST. Once you begin understanding how you cocreate interpersonal dramas, you may feel rather overwhelmed with self-awareness. Once I understood the FST, I saw it all over my life. Thankfully, it helped me respect others and trust that often when people react it is not personal at all. If their finite self is engaged, they are responding in defense, which is always from the finite self. That detachment brought me great peace. I no longer took everything personally. Once you identify how often people are just saying out loud what they are working on, it can help you witness their evolution. Additionally, I had assumed I was doing so much for others; however, many times they were absolutely unaware of my actions or it was none of my business. I would wait for their acknowledgment, but since they did not ask for my help, why would they thank me for something they did not need nor know I was doing? Once you gain perspective on why and where you step in, you can actually have a good giggle with yourself.

173

WITNESSING THE ROLES WE PLAY

To gain further insight, here are a few suggestions to understand the how and why of the FST roles you assume. We will play all of them, so you might want to prioritize which role you default to, what triggers the initiation, as well as how often you step into the other two roles.

When You Play Rescuer:

- Focus upon supporting and empowering the other person.

- Help by invitation only.

- Observe with the very feeling you are avoiding by stepping into the rescuer role. Go into your body and feel the feeling you are ignoring by focusing upon another person's needs. How does what they are feeling make you feel? Is it near a chakra? What color is the discomfort? What color would make that place feel better? Sit with the feeling of not knowing and nurture it with with your divine feminine self.

- Do not make their problem yours. No fixing allowed.

- Learn to say "no."

- You first. Honor your time and attention by setting limits on how much you will do. If this creates guilt, learn to love the feeling. What you give is enough, so practice giving only what is asked of you.

- Schedule your week fulfilling your needs. Make those appointments nonnegotiable and do not cancel them just because someone else needs you. Once you establish your schedule, make time for others in blocks of time, so you have a finish time. This way you are practicing boundaries.

- Track your resentment, guilt, and anxiousness. Find where you feel these things within your body and nurture that place with attention and color. If these feelings bring up moments from your past, explore them using the soul-centered insight exercise. If these emotions are beyond your ability to understand, find a practitioner to help you.

- Shape-shift into your divine feminine animal and become that ferocious loving mother who runs by instinct, trust, and connection to all that is. Let her teach you how to nurture and empower another into their becoming.

When You Play Victim:

- Connect to your "little you" and imagine you are helping yourself. What does that "little you" know about you that you have forgotten? Make it fun to not know.

- Define your needs and create a plan of action, even if it starts with baby steps.

- Draw, create, and use your imagination to feel what it would be like if you had what you wish. This part of us is little, so playtime is a must.

- Since victims will focus upon what is not working, go on a "negativity diet" and disallow yourself to say anything but positive statements. I did this with a client recently and once she was given this homework, she did not speak for a few minutes trying to find something to say. Celebrate your strengths. Anytime you say something negative or disempowering about yourself, first of all, do not start on a rage against yourself. Just stop, take a breath, and then say three things that are celebratory and empowering about yourself both in conversation and within your thoughts.

- Notice when you feel unable or incapable. Find that feeling inside your body and nurture that place. Feed it color and honor that you are so much more than you are remembering.

- When you feel resentment toward or disempowered by others when they succeed, practice congratulating or complimenting them. They do not diminish you, you do. They are showing you what success looks like, so you can learn from them. Imagine feeling how they feel and what that success would allow you.

175

- Research famous people who "made it" despite adverse circumstances. Abraham Lincoln had businesses fail, a fiancée die, had a nervous breakdown, ran for many offices and lost before becoming the 16th President of the United States. Our country would be so very different if he just gave up.

When You Act as a Persecutor:

- Focus upon connecting and speaking from your heart.

- Notice when you are completely in your mind. When you do, drop your attention back into your heart. Think of the elevator on your head and have "little you" take the elevator down to your heart and set up base camp.

- Notice when your anger pushes others away. Focus upon your soul seat to stay fully present with the other person.

- Nurture their becoming through your positive example. Recognize what strengths they possess by praising them and be willing to acknowledge where you are learning from them.

- Examine why you get defensive. What are you afraid of others knowing about you? Find that place within your body and explore that place fully. Find a healing color that calms and soothes your anger so when you get angry you can visualize that color around and within you. You can even imagine your words are colored with the healing color as you speak them.

- Be willing to be wrong and practice finding humor in your shortcomings.

- Shift into your divine masculine animal and find the loyal heart and dominion without dominating. Our masculine side is a soul-centered leader. Lead by example and help others see what walking your talk looks like.

By nurturing yourself through each of these exercises, you will begin to witness how much energy is expended unnecessarily when you defend, recoil, overdo, and overthink. Imagine what you can do with all the free time and energy you will regain by not getting involved in unnecessary tangles and theatrics. The exercise below focuses on transcending your most common FST role. Go to http://www.newharbinger.com/41849 to download the audio for it.

❋ EXERCISE ❋
Meditation to Nurture Your Default FST Role

Now that you know which FST role you step into, let's shift from the experience of the finite self to the wisdom of the infinite self. Our goal is to be so at peace with all the moments of our life that we can be fully present in this moment.

Imagine you are a "little you" standing on top of your head. You are perfect and playful and ready. An elevator door materializes in front of you. You walk inside and turn around. You decide to explore the feeling place that was activated by the role you play. The elevator descends. When the elevator doors open, you will be some place in nature where you are safe and loved. Let the elevator doors open now. When you are ready, step out into the natural landscape. You feel drawn to the water within this landscape. It may be a lake, pond, ocean, or river. Go to that place now. You can fast forward and just arrive there. Take in the water-filled place. Is it still, moving, flowing, or rushing? What do you notice about the water? Take a deep breath in and inhale the fresh, clean, moisture-filled air. Gently exhale. The water is shallow enough to wade into. As you look across the water, you notice a waterfall. Witness the calming mist that floats out from the descending water. Walk toward it now. Standing in front of the waterfall, feel the warm mist. Take in the sound of the water falling and crashing into the surface below. It is peaceful, rejuvenating, and relaxing.

Look into the waterfall and witness a figure just behind the falling water. As you examine it more fully, it is the "little you" from your childhood memory. See that part of you. What color do they need? Imagine a line of that colored light extending from your heart, through the water, into their heart. Feed their heart with color. Invite them into the waterfall, so you meet looking into each other's eyes underneath the water. Imagine the color of your heart line now colors the water. The falling colored water cleanses you both and then falls into the water below, coloring it with healing light. Bring your attention back to your past self and ask them what they know about you that you have forgotten. Listen to their wisdom. Feel the love between the two of your grow. In an instant, "little you" blends into your energy field and you become one. They are you and you are them.

You emerge from the waterfall and take in the surrounding landscape. How has it changed? How has the color shifted the feeling of the place? Look back upon the shore at your spiritual loved ones, guides, and pets that are creating the sacred space for this healing. Honor their presence. Receive their love. As you walk back toward the shore, look into the water. There you will find an energy gift. It may be an object, color, person, or guide. Whatever you discover, take it with you. Walk back to the shore and find the elevator. Step in and turn around. Press the top button. The doors close and you return to the top of your head. As the doors open, step out. Take a deep breath in and exhale. When you are ready, open your eyes.

Understanding the Gift

Take a few minutes to write down your observations from the above meditation. You might want to consider the following questions.

- Where did you find yourself in nature?

- What kind of water did you discover?

- What color did your soul desire?

- What did your past self say to you?

- Who was there supporting you?

- What was the gift you discovered?

Working with energy gifts can be very enlightening. Sometimes we will know right away what something means, but other times we can be quite confused by a gift. No matter what your reaction, shape-shifting can be used to explore anything energetic, including an object. The added benefit of this skill is that you do not need to meditate. It is like playing a game, because you become the object.

Let's say the gift I receive is an old-fashioned pen made from a feather that is dipped into an inkwell. I begin by becoming the pen. I use my soul feeling to help me empathically experience what that might feel like. I explore not just the object, but its function. I am a feather. What bird did I come from? This is not about being factually correct. I may envision I am a phoenix. Follow where your imagination takes you. After exploring the bird, I might ask: What does it feel like to be dipped into ink? Do I feel the creative energy of the writer as I am placed upon the paper? How does it feel to write letters and be so close to the creative process? What you will discover is the gift is giving you permission to step into your soul differently. For instance, this gift would be perfect for me writing this book. I would realize the spirit world would want to participate in the book's conversation and my job was just to implement their guidance. I am the feather. The feather could help me if I was overthinking to detach and listen to the spirit world. It could also be an invitation to take a break and go outside, where feathers might cross my path. The fun part is there is absolutely no right or wrong. The object holds many gifts, so give your finite mind a time out and let "little you" lead. Finally, talk as the object to you. What am I, the quill, teaching Austyn? What I know about Austyn that she need to know now?

You can use these meditations and exercises to explore each of the FST roles you engage. Just release any expectations of the finite self and surrender. It is fine if the place you return to is the same place as before. It is also perfect if the place the elevator takes you is totally different. Just trust what happens and enjoy. These processes are meant to be expansive, but most of all fun!

THE ENERGY BETWEEN US

Much like a baby connects to the mother through the umbilical cord, we also energetically connect to each other consciously and unconsciously. If someone were to cut that cord between mother and child too soon, the child would not live unless it was placed on some kind of life support. The child relies upon that cord to sustain itself and live until it is born, at which time the cord is cut and the child begins its own individual existence.

Using that analogy, our soul forms unions with people throughout our lives. Much like electrical cords, energy cords are simply lines of light or energetic information highways that connect one soul to another soul. We connect because we are learning from each other. Those cords exist between us and all the souls with whom we have relationships. We need these cords. When we finish the learning, the cord simply disconnects and disintegrates, because there is no longer a need for the connection.

We may not like who or what we are connected to. Some people will go to an energy practitioner and demand to be disconnected from a situation, person, place, or thing by having an energetic cord cut. Alternatively, energy workers may say they will cut your cords for you. If you have not finished your work around understanding why that situation is showing up and integrating what you are learning from it, those cords may be momentarily severed, but the minute you revisit the unfinished situation, they will reconnect. Cords are not bad or good; they are simply energy exchanges between souls. The idea is not to jettison or expel these connections we have with people or situations, but to try to understand *why* your soul would chose that person or experience and then integrate the blessings. These connections offer incredible insights. Once the lesson is understood and the wisdom gained, that cord will either release or be recharged and rejuvenated, reflecting the newly updated and healthy connection.

Humankind has such an amazing opportunity to exercise judgment or grace. We have enough to focus on within our own soul that judging and wishing ill upon others seems like such a waste of our soul's beauty. Our thoughts about others create connections. If we have anger or hate toward another, that energy will also be toxic for our soul and our physical form over time. We are responsible for all we do, including our thoughts and intentions even if they are only known to our souls. The goal is always to find the peace within ourselves and learn from who and what is around us.

As you transition out of the theatrics of the FST, you will begin to crave relationships that are equal, respectful, and empowering. The additional benefit is you will witness the roles others play. It will help you to be empathic to their process and understand who you have attracted to you and why. As you shift your engagement, be prepared that you may outgrow certain relationships while others strengthen. If you are evolving, so will the topography of your relationships. Always honor these souls for how they have contributed to your becoming and leave with gratitude. It is amazing how much you will crave self-awareness and mutual respect. Your transformation will create new pathways for future generations of your soul family to traverse. All it takes is one person to shift a family's karma. That is why you are so important, because you are the change.

CHAPTER 10

Honoring Grief, Loss, and Death

And she loved a little boy very, very much—
even more than she loved herself.

—Shel Silverstein, *The Giving Tree*

I was watching my friend and colleague Suzane Northrop demonstrate mediumship at the annual Afterlife Conference created by clinical chaplain and death educator Terri Daniel. Suzane was delivering a message to a client of mine, Lydia, and deeply connecting with her son Matthew in spirit. To conclude, she said Matthew wanted to acknowledge the lady who helped his mom know he was okay, as well as thank her for getting her to the conference. I almost fell out of my chair. Lydia first connected with Matthew's soul in a sitting we had earlier that year. Matthew was acknowledging he was aware not only of our mediumship sitting, but the fact that I was the reason his mom was even sitting in that room. That was the first time I got a message from a soul in spirit who I never met in the physical world.

A parent should never lose a child. For most of us, it is unthinkable; however, for such a parent, their grief does not end. It is a daily adjustment to a future they did not foresee. When my publishers asked me to include a chapter on grief and mourning, I could have shared my perceived wisdom as a medium and certified grief counselor. However, I realized the most delicate and powerful souls I know are the parents of children in the spirit world. This chapter is dedicated to three moms and their spirit boys. Each mom wanted me to use their real name, as well as their son's. No matter how a child dies, a parent will always want to talk about and honor them for all the ways their life mattered.

I asked each mom to talk about their son, their grief journey, and what they can teach us about how to walk our own journey of grief as well as support others who are mourning. Each of the stories is written by the mom in her own words. I intersperse some perspective and history throughout this chapter, but it is primarily a deep and truthful sharing from three very, very brave women.

DEANNA AND HER SON MATTHEW 183

I met Deanna at the same Afterlife conference referenced above. She is an amazing mom. Her son's name is Matthew. Here is their story.

> Eleven days before, Matthew came into my home office with joy and a sense of peace. He told me, "Mom, I finally know what I want to do with my life. I want to play music for others and make them feel the way I do when I play the piano—as if I have somehow touched my soul." "Soul" talk was not typical in our home, so this proclamation from Matt was unusual. It was, in retrospect, timely. I had no "sense" about Matthew before it happened. I do believe *he* did. I remember him telling me on more than one occasion that he would not live very long, that he would die before he was 27. Matthew was a heroin addict who rarely was in recovery. He had been living with me a few months now, since taking an official leave from college. I was always afraid to leave town, always afraid to leave him.

On April 30th, Matthew drove my mom and me to the airport. He and my father hugged us goodbye. He spent the day helping my dad in the yard. At one point he sent a group text to all his friends that read "What a beautiful day to be alive."

He died later that night of an accidental overdose at the age of 25.

May 1, I received a call from my husband. "Matthew was found on his bedroom floor." The rest is sharp and yet blurred at the same time. Painful to remember, yet difficult to forget. My husband's voice. My scream. I forced myself to scream because I couldn't get the attention of my family any other way. I slumped down to the ground. I screamed again. It was a hollow, forced scream. Within an hour we were back at the airport. Quietly holding hands on the airplane, my mother and I wanting to scream…but were forced into silence on this airplane. Tears pouring, yet we could not speak of it. We could not speak because we both knew we could not control ourselves. We needed to stay in control on this plane.

My next memory relevant to this journey was when a work friend came to the house and asked if I needed a Xanax. My immediate response was "No, Matthew will try to get in touch with me. I can't use any medication because Matthew will try." As I said this, I can still remember how resolute about this I was, as if it were common. Dead people were around, they could communicate, *and this one needed to reach out to me.* Only later did this seem peculiar.

—Deanna

WE MUST MOURN

Grief is the sorrow we feel when someone dies, however, mourning is the process that helps us work through our grief. We must mourn. We have to feel our lives without that soul and experience their absence in order to understand the power of love, as well as to process the depth of what remains within our heart that connects to their soul.

Grief is a very deep introspective experience. For some of us, this is the only time we feel the depth of our feelings regarding the soul who has died. What makes grief more solitary is our society's discomfort with the subject of death. It is a shared inevitability, yet we seem unable to articulate our feelings about it, much less support those we know and love who have lost someone they love.

To understand how death became such an invisible reality, we must look at the 1800s. Named after England's Queen Victoria, the Victorian Age coincided with the Industrial Age. This expansive time for American businesses gave birth to a new and healthy middle class. Their homes reflected great opulence to demonstrate their newly acquired status. One such example was the addition of the parlor. A purposefully showy room, it was filled with the family's best furniture and wares, as it was in this room that the neighbors, family, and friends would attend social events like births, weddings, and also funerals.

185

In the northern American rural towns, church bells would toll a recognized Morse code when someone died providing the deceased person's age and gender. Funeral processions traveled through most of the town and the burial grounds were sometimes in the city's center right next to the town church. Death was part of daily life and shared by the community.

When someone died, the family members wore specific clothing, so the community could recognize someone had died. The coffin was either homemade or purchased at the general store. The body was placed in an open coffin and brought to the parlor. Different family members were assigned a constant 24-hour watch, inspiring the term "wake." This was to make sure that the person was actually dead, not just in a coma or sleeping. The wakes were three to four days long, allowing family and friends to travel to the family home to gather, commiserate, and mourn together in the parlor along with that soul's body. Flowers and candles were present to mask any unpleasant odors.

As photography was increasingly more affordable, photos were also taken, not just of family and friends, but of the dead. Called *memento mori*, Latin for "remember you must die," these photos depicted the loved one with their eyes painted open on the finished photographs so they could be remembered as if in life. Many of the photographs were of children because the infant mortality rate was about 20 percent of live births, and 10 percent of children did not live to see their 21st birthday. Although we honored our dead more visibly, it was certainly not without fear.

There are all sorts of superstitions that arose from having a dead person in the house. The windows of the home were covered with dark or white material, as well all pictures and mirrors. This way the spirit could not get stuck or remain within the reflective surfaces. People wore black to appear as shadows, not visible bodies that could be inhabited by the newly transitioned spirit.

The body was removed from the home through a door in the parlor, always feet first, so the spirit not only left the home, but did not take anyone else's soul with them into the spirit world. There were many who felt it was bad luck to take the body out the front door, as it might curse the house.

Yet it was the Civil War that truly altered our communal practices of death. This was the first time our country experienced deaths away from home. As the dead soldiers had to be transported long distances to be returned to their families, death specialists treated the bodies with a new procedure called embalming, which allowed the body to maintain a lifelike appearance and decompose at a much slower rate. Also, more attention was paid to the appearance of the body, inspiring many to experiment with different preservation techniques. This created an emergence of funeral directors and homes, makeup artists, insurance agencies, cemeteries, florists, automobile companies making hearses, and coffin manufacturers. Death became an industry as Americans stepped into the second Industrial Age.

American workers moved from hand tools to machines and automation. Institutions like hospitals emerged so when our family became ill they were more likely to be taken to hospitals to be cared for and treated rather than being visited by a family physician at home. When someone died, they now seemed to disappear. Someone else tended, prepared, and buried our family members. Death shifted from a visible intimate familial experience to an impersonal, and almost invisible, event.

Fortunately, today there are many practitioners providing services to allow a more intimate and private death experience. There are death doulas, death midwives, home and green funeral officiates and celebrants available to help you and your family and friends create personalized death ceremonies and facilitate conversations around death. Our fear of death has increased, because it has become more impersonal. We need to return to talking, seeing, and embracing our grief and death as well as our own mortality.

LYDIA AND HER SON MATTHEW

When I first sat with Lydia, I had the hardest time not laughing out loud because her spirit son Matthew kept bouncing all over the room. I said, "Your son says he is a monkey, like Curious George, because he was getting into everything." This was significant because Matthew was buried wearing his Curious George tie. In spirit, Matthew has been a dutiful son. Matthew has helped his mom through her grief, helped her find missing objects, and is always around when she needs his love. I believe it was Matthew's soul who instigated the lifelong friendship that Lydia and I share.

Sometimes people die in accidents because of the negligence of others. We will want to blame the instigators. We can experience tremendous anger of the suddenness of our loved one's death. We can have many unanswered questions, few of which may be answered. In such cases, our grief can additionally be compounded if we must attend lengthy trials to seek justice for our loved ones. Here is Lydia and Matthew's story.

Many of my major life shifts were a result of decisions I had made. Marriage, children, moving cross-country, and even illnesses were occurrences that seemed logical and a natural part of our lives. The death of our son is one puzzle piece that doesn't fit. Matthew was born too early at only six months' gestation, weighing in at just over two pounds. He came home with oxygen tanks and heart monitors. I felt blessed that he survived and even thrived.

He was whimsical, spoke to strangers readily, and loved the Renaissance Festivals. He fell in love and married. Matthew's wife was seven months pregnant when the police showed up in their driveway. It was October 13, 2007, 11 days shy of Matthew's 24th birthday. A driver in a van next to Matthew's jeep crossed into his lane. When Matthew swerved to avoid a collision, his jeep went into the median strip, flipped, and he died instantly.

When his wife called me after the accident, I made her repeat the words "he didn't make it" several times, because I was *sure* I hadn't heard her right. The young driver in the van who caused the accident saw Matthew's jeep flip in his rearview mirror, called 911 anonymously, and kept driving. Witnesses recorded his plate number. Months later in court he spoke about driving the van for his church. He wanted to study law and positively impact the world. During Matthew's trial, he entered an Alford plea asserting his innocence instead of the "guilty" plea we were told to expect. Upon this pronouncement, both the judge and my husband looked at me for direction. I was exhausted. We'd already been through so much. Nothing could change what had transpired. We didn't argue; we accepted his plea.

Having a child is a blessing. If your child dies, you have been robbed of that blessing. If your child dies, you feel like you have "lost" your child and failed at your responsibility to keep them safe. Many parents who have lost a child feel that they either need to be punished (through dying also) or follow their children to continue their parental role (through suicide).

I search for the meaning in my children's lives. What has each child taught me? In the unfolding of Matthew's tragedy, I consider our family to be blessed in many ways. Our son did not suffer. We were supported by friends and family. We thanked God that Matthew's wife and unborn child were not in the car with him. We had the privilege of watching our son grow and fall in love. And we have a beautiful granddaughter. I have to remind myself that I had a life before Matthew and I have a life after Matthew. No matter how much I love him, his earthly existence is over for now; mine is not.

UNCHARTED TERRITORY

Grief has no pattern or logic. You cannot control how you navigate the landscape of your grief. You can feel emotions of shock, denial, rage, loneliness, guilt, fear, anxiety, and apathy. You might become defiant, detached, childlike, uncontrollably emotional, and numb. The best you can do is take it day by day. Be honest about your needs and feelings. Let people help.

189

Death will make you deeply review your life. You will question what you believe, what you have been taught, and what you think you know. You may find yourself contemplating eternity, as well as whether there is heaven or hell. This is part of the process. You are allowed to change your mind about what you believe. In your early life, you were surrounded by others' beliefs that may have become your own. Part of the authentication of your soul is asking questions and discovering your own truth. Death is a great equalizer and educator, because it reminds us that this existence is temporary and none of us knows how long we will live.

WHY CAN'T I FEEL MY LOVED ONES?

People often remark that they are unable to sense their loved ones after they have died. One possible reason for this is that when we grieve, we are in our finite self. Since your emotions and mind are overwhelmed, your infinite self can feel less accessible. Without that soul connection, we have the impression that our loved ones are not present. Nothing could be further from the truth. The spirit world has told me it is as if they are behind a window, witnessing our experience. Our thoughts are lines of light that penetrate and reach their soul. They know when we are thinking of them. Imagine your senses are completely aware and open, so that you can feel any vibration or signal that comes from someone you love. As we mourn and our finite mind processes our grief, we can begin to feel them more and more. It is magical when their soul breaks through the clouds of our thoughts and grief. They remind us their love is eternal.

SON SIGNS

Lydia

On the night of Matthew's car accident, a family friend drove Lydia home from his house after visiting with his wife. Severe fatigue and numbness began to set in. As they turned the corner toward a fast-food place, in front of them was a jeep, just like Matthew's. The license plate read LOOK4ME.

A few days later, after making funeral arrangements, Lydia and her husband noticed another license plate which read JOHN 14:27. The Bible passage reads, "Do not let your hearts be troubled, and do not let them be afraid."

Years later, they were on a Florida nature tour. A young man walked up to ask the guide a question. Lydia jumped back. He was Matthew's doppelganger. Everything about this young man, from his facial features and mannerisms down his bucket hat, T-shirt, and cargo pants, was the exact likeness of her son. When Lydia texted her daughter pictures of this young man, even she believed it was her brother. Lydia kept taking pictures of the alligators and turtles nearby just to capture this man's image. As she did this, a single white feather floated toward her. She saw that as a sign from her son. Just as I finished writing this section of the chapter and walked out of my office, a single white feather was in the middle of my hallway.

Deanna

Two years after her son overdosed, Deanna's mother died. Her mom had been a tower of strength for her. The last thing Deanna requested from her mother before she died was to give her a sign when she found Matthew. Within 30 minutes of her death, the family heard the cooing of a mourning dove inside the house. It was so loud they thought it was inside the chimney. It stayed for over half an hour. The dove became their sign when Matthew and his grandmother's soul were present.

The entire time I have written this chapter, a single mourning dove has been sitting in a tree outside my window. We do not normally have mourning doves in our area.

Later that same year, Deanna learned her daughter had become pregnant. Almost immediately, a mourning dove and its partner flew into Deanna's view and cooed.

Five days before her due date, opting to work with a doula, Deanna's daughter's water broke without contractions. Matthew's sister proclaimed she could feel the baby's head. Instead of running into Deanna's bedroom, which had been the plan, she ran with the doula in tow to Matthew's old room. Her beautiful baby boy Max was born in the exact spot where Matthew had died. He was born on Deanna's mom's birthday.

COMMON EXITS AND ENTRANCES

The spirit world has told me when two different people are born or die on the same date, their souls are linked. They can share similar lessons or personalities. Much like a funnel appears above our crown chakra, a similar shape or wormhole exists when a soul enters or exits this world. This passage portal is an exit in time and space, like a freeway off-ramp. When a soul has already entered or exited on that date, it is a potential exit portal for future souls' births or deaths.

We also have multiple potential exit points within our life, meaning your soul has a number of moments that you could potentially die. Sometimes those exit points exist so if you cannot transcend a certain lesson, you have an option to leave this world. As we work through our karma, sometimes we will transcend a possible exit point. This could account for the "close calls" some people experience.

According to the Substance Abuse and Mental Health Services Administration, about sixty percent of youths from ages 12 to 17 with a major depressive episode do not receive treatment for their depression (Tice 2017). With the rise of gun-related deaths in our schools and bold pleas from the youth of our country to effect positive change, mental illness demands our attention and action. Before I met Mary, I was unaware of the journey a parent can experience when dealing with mental health issues that can often lead to suicide. Her story follows.

MARY AND HER SON BEN

Losing someone to suicide, or any other sudden, traumatic death, is painful by itself. For most parents of teenage or young adult suicides, the first glimpse that something is wrong is when their child kills themself. It's more complicated when the death is preceded by another kind of loss, when the person you once knew also dies. One never gets over a loss like mine. I prefer to think of grief like organic matter on the soil of my soul. It assimilates into who I am and makes me richer in many ways. I never forget the pain of the loss but as I gain perspective, the sting isn't as visceral.

If Ben had taken his life a year earlier, I would have assigned blame for his actions on something logical like a life event such as a break-up with a girlfriend or loss of a job. I wouldn't have known the raging battle with voices and thoughts that came from places foreign to the essence of the soul I brought into this world. Ben was a social butterfly. He was kind, clever, and had a great sense of humor. However, after the 9/11 attacks, he ran away from school because he was afraid. Another time, his vice principal coaxed Ben out of his car. He sat in her office terrified the rest of the day. A very kind, sensitive psychiatrist started Ben on antidepressants and the school agreed to send teachers to the house while he recovered.

Ben was in and out of school because his brain was like a roller coaster being pulled up that steep incline by the antidepressants. His speech was fast, he didn't sleep, he began getting into fights, and his behavior became erratic. The doctor shifted him off the antidepressants, replacing them with antipsychotics, but the medicine didn't help. Ben's disruptions were unpredictable and he became more violent. I was losing sleep trying to figure out how to help him.

I found a spiral notebook in his room filled with violent thoughts and drawings that included rape, murder, and senseless rambling. The edges of each page were lined with the ABCs. I wondered who Ben was becoming. He was a good boy.

One night in April, I was trying to get Ben to go to sleep as he fidgeted and rambled. He asked me if I would lie down with him and I said I would sit with him while he fell asleep. He looked at me and said, "I know you have sex with my brother. Now it's our turn." I assured Ben that I loved him deeply, but not like that. Ben had become increasingly obsessed with sex. He pulled the covers down to expose himself. I told him to cover himself. I left him in his room, abruptly rushing to mine. As I opened my bedroom door to stop his knocking, 6'2" Ben stood staring at me and he said, "You know what I want." This lasted for four hours until I left to stay at my mother's house. I prayed that he wouldn't take his life.

The next day he was hospitalized. During admission, Ben identified people that he wanted to kill and the police had to notify the parents of these other children. Someone at the hospital told Ben he would be able to smoke, but when he was denied, he hammered his right hand into a cement wall, moving the last three knuckles on his hand into his wrist. It took over a week in the psych ward before they felt he was mentally stable enough to have the necessary surgery to hold his hand together.

One day in the hospital, I asked him if he was okay. He looked at me earnestly and said, "Mom, it is so hard to ignore what's going on in my head." A few seconds later he hissed, "Why are you here?"

By the time he was released from the hospital, he was on lithium. He slept a lot. He complained that he felt dull and his vocabulary was stunted. His hands shook so much that he couldn't keep food on his fork. His social anxiety increased so he couldn't be out in public without feeling the need to rush home. The doctors continued to try to find the right medicine, but his brain never found solid ground.

The medication affected his ability to "perform," so he referred to that as "his problem."

On July 19, 2002 at the age of 17 years old, I lost my son. He died by suicide. I found him. He hung himself.

Ben left three suicide notes. The first read:

"Why did I kill myself? Because I am alone and will always be alone because of my problem. I am scared of going to hell."

The second note read: "Dear God, I am suffering so much here. Please forgive me. Amen."

The third note simply said, "I am sorry Mom."

Mary was kind enough to share with me her journal entries after Ben died. When someone takes their life, the lack of closure creates profound confusion, guilt, fear, and sadness. I am grateful for her courage and transparency.

JOURNAL ENTRIES FROM BEN'S MOM AFTER HIS DEATH

One Month Later

We lost Ben. I lost my son—my youngest. The grief is unbearable and life will never be the same. I feel as though

I'm lost in a fog with no senses. I torture myself with ways I could have prevented it. If only I had stayed home that day; if only I had insisted he go to the hospital when he vocalized his suicidal thoughts. Why didn't the doctor suggest it when I called him? Did I trust the wrong doctor? Questions assail me and there are no answers—except my Ben is gone. How can that be? I remember thinking, as I was driven to his funeral, that it was the first time in a long time that I wasn't worried about where he was and what he was doing. The worst had happened. Maybe not the worst…he could have taken others with him and that would have been horrible.

Three Months Later

I don't remember writing the last entry. It's all a blur. It seems so unreal to say "Ben died," "Ben's funeral," "Ben's death." I made the first flower arrangement for his grave a couple weeks ago. It was a beautiful fall arrangement in a brass container. "His grave"—another phrase.

Four Months Later

My thoughts are still consumed with grief and loss. I see Ben as I found him several times a day. Thoughts of him and the loss of him are the last thing on my mind when I go to sleep—along with my plea and prayers to God for healing and peace. He is among the first thoughts I have as I greet each day—it's always a letdown when I realize he's really not here. And even though I "know" he is with God and I will see him again—I feel deprived of knowing him more fully here on earth. The loss has no boundaries. The grief touches all parts of me. I miss Ben so much.

Eleven Months Later

Ben—I miss you. I love you. I am afraid I will get used to life without him. I was 29 when Ben was born—he was 17 when he died. I've already lived longer than the length of time I knew him. I don't want to be happy again because it might mean I've forgotten my dear Ben. The pain of missing him is—and has been—so strong. If the pain of grief subsides, will I forget?

Letter to Ben on the Second Anniversary of His Death

My dear Ben, it's been two years since you left. I cry a lot. It hurts so much and it remains so fresh. The pain sometimes eclipses the joy that comes with living and loving. I still look forward to that final journey when I see you again. I know that's wrong thinking, but it's there. My mind wanders back. I look at the pictures and try to determine when you began the descent. Why didn't I see it? Why did I not respond with more caution? Why couldn't I save you and spare you such pain? I would've moved heaven and earth if I could have— and I didn't…I couldn't…and it all comes down to this…you are gone. You are "there" waiting for me to find you. My worst fear was realized. You took your life. How could you do that? I told you it would kill me and you promised you wouldn't and I believed you. We were all so tired. You've been fighting a horrific battle. You were intense. I can't make sense of it and I don't know what else to do with my pain but to write you about it and cry and pray like I do every single day for healing. FYI: I'm the little boy on the front of this card wanting to be with you again. I love you—Mom.

WISDOM FROM DEANNA, LYDIA, AND MARY

Deanna, Lydia, and Mary are heroes to me. I marvel at their tenacity, optimism, raw honesty, and faith. Therefore, I asked them to help all of us with how we can better grieve and mourn.

What helped you get through your grief?

Deanna: I read absolutely everything I could about the afterlife, near-death experiences, and reincarnation, including self-help books, channeled writings, and those written by mediums. Our family and friends received signs from Matthew through dreams, messages, photographs, and signs. I reached out to other parents who lost a child. I found comfort in gatherings with like-minded people. I have received a few readings by mediums over the years.

Lydia: I listened to music, including new music. I needed to avoid musical artists that I associated with my lost child. I watched old movies, because they do not contain the violence, sex, and rough language that movies have now. It gave my mind rest from worry, analysis, guilt, remorse, and grief. I prayed for strength, as well as for other families who had lost children or are in great need. I found meditation comforting. After Matthew died, I started ending my emails with "Be Well, Be Happy, Be Thankful" because it reminded me to care for myself and focus on the good times. I love talking about Matthew. He loved to dress up in costumes even as an adult. He taught me a lot about not taking life too seriously.

Mary: If the loss is fresh, just breathe. Do what is needed to get through the day. Be gentle with yourself. Find a way to express feelings of loss and sadness, as well as ways to celebrate life. I wrote cards to Ben as well as my thoughts in a journal. I read books about suicide, mental illness, and grief. I found peace in tending Ben's grave. I participate in an annual Bereaved Parents memorial each December where Ben's picture is shown. We each light a candle when our child's name is read. I have stayed in touch with Ben's friends. I love it when I hear a new story about him. By spending time with them, I can see the age he would have been and what he might have been involved with through his friends' lives. I have become close to other families whose children died by suicide. I garden and love my pets. It was a healing revelation when I realized Ben was truly with me. I also send love to all the families whose children die, including the children whose mental illness leads to the death of other children.

How can we best support people who are grieving?

Deanna: Do attend the wake and/or funeral! I say this because I rarely attended wakes and would sit way in the back at a funeral if I went at all, thinking my presence was unneeded. Not so. I may not remember half the people who were at Matthew's wake and funeral, but I do remember the crowds. This was so comforting.

Do visit and bring food. I may not need constant companionship, but I did like the distraction. The food helped me feel less guilty knowing there was food for my family.

I loved when Matthew's friends came to visit and tell stories. His little brother particularly needed this. Even a few months later, my son would cling to every word. We love keeping in touch with Matt's friends.

Do ask me about Matthew. Write me a note that you're thinking about me, suggest a book that may help. I needed it all.

Please don't ask me if I am *better*. I am not sick, and I will not ever feel *better*.

Don't tell me "Time heals all wounds."

Do not tell someone you are glad they are "moving on." Just last week I posted on Facebook that I was finally ready to sell Matthew's piano. Not a day before would I have been ready and that's okay, however I decide to do things on my schedule. There is no right or wrong. I am not "moving on." I'm just moving.

I do believe that time *changes* grief. Time was my enemy, really. I couldn't see a future in which I had to endure such pain for any length of time, I hope that I will have more good days and fewer bad ones. I do believe that 20 years from now, I could still suddenly become overcome with loss—a pain so deep that it feels as enormous as that first day.

Lydia: DO—Share your memories of the deceased person with others. My son was a goofball. Friends told me funny stories of his lighthearted nature. Memories are so healing.

DO—Especially in the early days, offering to take care of mundane chores is welcome. Picking up something at the grocery store, straightening up the kitchen, yard work. With the initial shock comes numbness, making everyday tasks difficult.

DO—Remember anniversaries/birthdays if you can. This is a very nice way to show the bereaved that their loved one is not forgotten. It also shows that they are not alone in their memories. Other people continue to think of and pray for their lost loved one.

DO—Offer resources (grief groups, professional counseling) if the grief is complicated or drags on.

DO—Ride the waves of noise and quiet. There will be times when the person wants to talk, talk, talk. Listen. There will be times when there are no words to possibly capture the emotions. Be with your friend in the silence.

DO—My sister who lives one hour away sent me a funny card every Friday for a year. It lifted my spirits and let me know she was there for me if I needed her. It was such a nice, gentle thing. Simple cards, letters, email, text messages, all let them know you are thinking of them.

DO—Cry with me. It's okay. You don't have to be strong for me. If you start crying, don't apologize. Showing your vulnerability lets me know I'm not alone in my pain.

DON'T—Overdo the helping. If you launch into a major housecleaning or take over the person's life, it could instill guilt.

DON'T—Smother. There is a delicate balance between letting the person know you are there for them and hovering over them trying to help.

DON'T—Quote platitudes. "It was meant to be." "It was part of God's plan." "It happened for a reason." Especially, "I know exactly how you feel!" Then recount *your* latest loss. You do not know nor will ever know how they feel, unless they tell you.

DON'T—Push the person to get on with life (get back to work or get busy to keep their mind off it). Only a grief counselor can determine if the bereaved is stalled in complicated grief.

DON'T—Try to answer why. Realize that the question of "Why?" is a haunting one that engenders analysis. It is a question that will never be answered. No one can answer it and don't try to.

DON'T—Avoid talking about the person who died. The situation isn't going away. Avoiding the subject only shows fear.

DON'T—Think that they'll "get over it." There is no timeline for grief. Just because time passes, the pain remains. They may be dealing with it better, but it doesn't go away.

Mary: Listen. If you are with someone else who has lost someone, the most important thing to do is listen. Allow the mourner to tell the story of the one who died, expressing the varied emotions. As a listener, you are saying, "Teach me about your grief and what you are experiencing."

Allow silence and stillness. After Ben died, I sometimes went to my mom's house and sat in the same room with her while she watched TV. I can't remember the shows. I just felt comfort being in the room with her and not talking.

Be supportive. We need to feel grief, express grief, and be around supportive people.

What would you say if someone who lost a loved one wanted to "join them"?

Lydia: I would say I understand.

Deanna: I would say I completely understand. I have been there. There are days when the pain of his loss is overwhelming and death seems somehow easier. However, I would remind them that they still have work to do and that the person they love is near them, guiding, and very much wants them to finish their work on earth. I would tell them there are lessons to be learned and the gifts will unfold in due time. I would invite them to take this journey with me—a spiritual journey. The journey where I speak to my son or my mother and I *know* they hear me, when I pray I *know* I am heard, when I receive a sign there is no doubt where it came from. It's a magical, mystical, beautiful journey I am on. There is room for everyone. I would tell them they have a choice.

Mary: It's normal to feel that way. I have felt that way. I've met others who have felt that way. Keep putting one foot in front of the other and eventually you learn to enjoy living again. If the thoughts become persistent and more concrete where there is a plan and more specific thoughts of suicide, then see someone professional and get help.

ANTICIPATORY GRIEF

When someone we love becomes ill and we foresee they could die, we experience what is called anticipatory grief. We will feel all the emotions we normally experience upon a person's death, on top of the physical and emotional exhaustion that occurs when we watch our loved one in the dying process. We will witness their gradual loss of independence, physical agility, personality, memory, and material stability and security. We will be hypervigilant about potential hazards and outcomes that may lead or contribute to their death, engaging the finite mind and putting the body into a constant state of fight-or-flight. If we are caregiving and supporting the person dying, our already apparent exhaustion will be exacerbated. The unexpected part of this kind of grief is when our loved one dies, we will feel understandable relief, which makes many feel profoundly guilty. The goal is to let our infinite self help us stay focused on the gift of their presence, attend to any unfinished business, and focus upon how we can support their soul and ours during this difficult time.

201

Being with someone who is dying can be intense, but it is also a tremendous gift. It is a great opportunity for us to listen to them and witness this change. Most people who are dying will want to talk about death. It is not a scary conversation, just one we do not practice. Besides taking care of the medical and legal issues around a person's property, there are ways you can support that person quite profoundly. You can ask who they would like with them when they die. How would they like their funeral? Hearing is the last sense we lose. Although that sense is highly sensitive around death, perhaps there is some music that they would love to have lightly present in the background. Talk about your fears and their fears around death.

Take time to celebrate who they are and how they have touched this world. Ask them what they are most proud of or what regrets they have. If there is a way to take action steps to tie up any loose ends, help them write a letter or call a friend and acknowledge their feelings and regrets. So much of my work as a medium is healing the relationships that were left unfinished. Take the time to have soul conversations and tell them all the ways your soul is better because they have lived. Tell them you love them as you are sharing a very vulnerable and solitary experience with them. If you have things to express, please do so. If there is anything on a bucket list that can be accomplished, make those plans.

Find ways their soul can be part of the future. They can write letters for future events or celebrations. Definitely talk about ways you can communicate after they die. Come up with signs and symbols so you will know their soul is at peace. Most of all, listen deeply to them and cherish the time you do have. Whether it is silent or in conversation, death is a beautiful and magical passage and offers great windows into what lies beyond.

HOW TO HONOR YOUR LOVED ONES HERE AND IN THE SPIRIT WORLD

Please take the time to keep your relationships in order. Apologize, say how you feel, and most of all, cherish the souls you wander this world with, no matter how challenging your relationship. Most of us assume we will grieve the most for those we are most bonded to. Ironically, it is often the more challenging and unresolved relationships we have with people who die that compound our grief. We become so accustomed to the drama of our shared relationship that their death can create a large void. Some will find another person to transfer the drama upon just because it is comfortable. When we take the time to learn from our relationships, even the dying process is easier for all parties concerned.

One of the best gifts I ever gave my parents was a large journal that I filled with questions for them to answer about their lives. For instance, I asked my dad about his service in the Aleutian Islands, if he was scared, how it felt being a father, and what made him most proud. I asked if he could have a dinner party with anyone from history, who would be there and why. If I had minutes to grab my most precious possessions, those books that my mom and dad filled out would be in my arms. I have their handwriting, stories and their voice, but most of all, I feel like I am sitting with their souls and listening to the story of their life. For my mom, I had her draw faces and moments. She included poetry she loves, and I discovered a number of things about her that I had lacked the curiosity to unearth.

We have days like Veterans' Day and Martin Luther King Day to honor collective souls and great souls who touched our nation. However, on a personal level, we would be well served to have a single day to remember and acknowledge our personal loved ones and the powerful impact a single soul has upon our lives.

Begun in Mexico, Día de los Muertos or Day of the Dead is celebrated all over Latin America. Each year for two days, generally November 1st and 2nd, departed children and loved ones are celebrated with colorful altars honoring their favorite food, drink, pictures, hobbies, and habits. There is a palpable whimsy in these altars. Family and friends gather and the days are spent remembering, mourning, and celebrating their souls. Sugar skulls or *calaveras* are decorated to honor the dead. Many elaborately paint their faces as skulls with tremendous artistry. This holiday is not to be confused with Halloween. Halloween is fear inspiring. Día de los Muertos is a celebration honoring the power of life and death. This celebration is just one of many such traditions that exist all over the world.

To honor your loved ones, you can create a simple altar in your home inspired by Día de los Muertos. Take your loved one's pictures and mementos and create a sacred place where they can be honored. You can add candles and flowers. Mostly, it allows you a place and space to acknowledge their souls.

Lastly, there are so many things you can do to honor your loved ones. People get tattoos celebrating their loved ones' souls. Ashes can be put into glass for necklaces and sculptures. Stars can be named, and trees and gardens can be planted. Money can be contributed to charities, and foundations and scholarships can be started. Some people run marathons or dedicate benches and plaques in honor of their loved ones. You can make quilts out of their clothing, frame their favorite team jersey, or make a collage honoring their passions through pictures.

There are people who come into hospitals offering photographic services for parents whose babies die. The photos I have witnessed are breathtaking and shot with incredible respect and love. You can create yearly commemorations with floating memorials, lantern and balloon releases for birthdays, anniversaries, and death dates. Bring pictures, mementos, or wear your loved one's jewelry to include them at weddings, holidays, and birthdays. Make ornaments or jewelry to celebrate their soul. It is especially fun in my mediumship sittings when departed loved ones talk about being in the room or at the party. Your souls shared much when they were alive, but they love being part of your life now.

Although death is a difficult experience, it is also filled with grace, miracles, unexpected humor, and love. Become the one in your family who initiates soul conversations about death and dying. In 2010, inspired by the work of Bernard Crettaz, Jon Underwood created Death Café, nonprofit meetings to facilitate discussions about death. I participated on a panel for a Death Café and found the experience healing, enlightening, and powerful. Beyond learning to talk about death, we all can be responsible by getting our own affairs in order. Allocate what you have and where it needs to go. Provide passwords and security information or keys. Allow your end of life wishes to be known. Most of all, communicate from your soul so when your death approaches, you will be as organized and prepared as possible. That way, your family and friends can be allowed to grieve and celebrate your life, without the distraction of your unfinished business.

CHAPTER 11

Exploring the Eternity of Your Soul

The known is finite, the unknown infinite; intellectually we stand on an islet in the midst of an illimitable ocean of inexplicability. Our business in every generation is to reclaim a little more land.

—T. H. Huxley

Mankind has always sought to define and quantify time. Our ancestors witnessed the repetitions of the seasons, as well as the movements of the sun and moon. The Sumerians created the first calendar over 5,000 years ago consisting of a yearlong calendar of 12 30-day months. Unfortunately, the disparity between the actual time the earth takes to rotate the sun and their mathematical observations produced a calendar that was off by almost a week. The Egyptians had the right idea to adjust this oversight. They just added a few extra days of celebration to the end of each year. Many cultures observed the movements of the moon, devising a lunar calendar. This proved equally problematic as it was also too short, resulting in the seasons falling out of sync.

According to NASA, the earth finishes a complete rotation around the sun in 365.2422 days (2018). Since our calendar is counted in whole numbers, we gain extra time each year. How do we make up for it? Leap years. But every century we have over-calculated by a full day, so in century years—1800, 1900—there is no leap year; that is, unless the year is divisible by four, like 2000, and then we add the leap year back in. As you can see, even our conventional framework for time necessitates leaps and changes.

The organization of time originated as a way to organize our connection to the natural world. However, our current relationship is more stressful because time is like quicksilver, elusive and difficult to grasp.

THE TEST OF TIME

To illustrate how unique we all are in our perceptions of time, please get a piece of paper and your favorite writing instrument. The following two exercises will explore your relationship with time.

❁ EXERCISE ONE ❁
Your View of Time

Everyone envisions time differently. You may see something very literal like a clock or a calendar or something more abstract like a circle or graph. The important thing is to capture exactly how you see time in your mind. Begin by imagining all the months of a year starting with January. How does that appear in your mind? Relax into the exercise. Draw the image you envision. Once you finish that drawing, capture different kinds of time: a minute, day, and a month. There is absolutely no wrong or right in this exercise.

When you have finished, take a look at your drawings. How are each of the units of time similar? How are they different? What has inspired how you envision time?

✺ EXERCISE TWO ✺
Emotions and Time

Answer the following questions.

1. What adjectives describe your view of time? Fast, slow, short, long…

2. When do you lose time?

3. How does time stress you? What do you do when you feel this way?

4. When are you pressed for time?

5. What do you not make time for?

6. When do you have too much time?

✺

207

THE TIME OF YOUR LIFE

Having a good relationship with time and witnessing when we let time create stress will assist you greatly. Our infinite self knows we have all the time we need. It is our finite self that perceives a limited view of time.

Our elusive relationship with time is reflected in the idioms we use in our everyday conversations. We race against time or have a good, hard, rare old, rough, or whale of a time. We can have too much time on our hands, be up against the clock, or simply have no time. We need time to breathe or think. We kill time, make time, have quality time, take time off, but there is no time like the present. Time heals all wounds, flies, drags, is short, long, ripe, borrowed, lost, found, yet waits for no man. We give kids a time out, but we get time off for good behavior. We are in the right place at the right time, stand the test of time, but the third time is the charm and time is money, so time is up.

Time is understood as the fourth dimension, after longitude, latitude, and altitude. Yet we perceive time more like a single dimension or a straight line. This rather inflexible view puts our past behind us like statues impervious to change and our future looming ahead of us with our present available only when we are not looking backward or ahead. The challenge with this perception is it makes time inflexible, so what has happened is set and what will happen is fated. We frequently project our past onto the future, and therefore approach upcoming moments with palpable trepidation. Since death is a topic our culture rarely embraces, future time can also be laced with fear because it hints at our mortality.

SOUL TIME

The spirit world has a completely different relationship with time. From their perspective, we have just the right amount of time to do what we need to do. Time is a space our soul expands into to discover ourselves within. During my mediumship sittings, souls in the spirit world remember the past and comment upon the present yet seem keenly aware of our future. However, their discussions indicate our future is not just a single destination, but rather contains an expanse of multiple destinies and possibilities. The spirit world often shows me future children, shares names of future partners, mentions surprise family events, and discusses happenings well before their occurrence. I receive emails from clients who revisit a past sitting recording only to discover what was not known at the time of the reading is now remarkable valid and currently applicable. The spirit world never mentions time with worry; in fact, I have not heard the spirit world talk about fearing anything. Time is expansive, hopeful, and creative.

❋ EXERCISE THREE ❋
Timelessness

What activities, hobbies, creative ventures, or people help you lose track of time? Perhaps you create, play music, sing, dance, act, or play a sport. This sensation can also be felt when you are with someone you love, a newborn, a pet, a romantic partner, or a friend. Choose the strongest activity or person from the list above and simply imagine that is what you are doing or who you are with now. Let your soul senses open up. Once the feeling is heightened, notice where within your body the energy of passion, creativity, or love is most evident in your soul. Scan your entire physical form and notice how many places you sense passion. How does your soul space feel around you? Be that "little you" and watch what it looks like when you are deeply connected to something or someone you love. Are there colors, images, or symbols within your soul space? What sounds or sensory perceptions come into your awareness? Open your senses to anything and everything. Once you have captured the experience, gently come back and open your eyes.

209

Take your paper and draw what you experienced. Allow it to capture any symbols, images, colors, shapes, abstracts, or movement that you witnessed. Take whatever time you need.

Compare the first time drawing, seeing time from the finite self, with this last drawing, envisioning from the soul.

Time is a great tool. We need a sense of organization and structure to understand how we move through our lives. However, when we let time rule us, we will always be in our finite self feeling stressed and overwhelmed. The idea is to create balance and have times when we explore timelessness or soul time.

❋

EMBRACING TIMELESSNESS

The journey into the soul can render people speechless, because language fails to capture the beauty and depth of what is perceived. This is why we have poetry, music, painting, writing, sculpting, dancing, singing, and so many other magical creations. The soul is always awaiting those moments when it can surrender, express authentically, and swim in eternal ethers of timelessness.

To help gain that sense of timelessness more often in your life, it helps to practice allowing our finite self to detach and our infinite self to navigate. This can be done by relaxing into a deeper level of consciousness.

To drop into slower brain states, we must shift from the finite self into the soul. This is done by relaxing your brain.

When our brain is in its everyday normal functioning, its level of alert consciousness is called "beta." Within that state, our rational and analytical mind emits 14 to 40 Hz or brain waves per second. In this state we can experience restlessness, anxiety, and stress, which is why consciously relaxing the brain has great physical, mental, and emotional benefits.

When we daydream, we are in a light trance of the alpha state of brain activity where the waves are eight to 14 waves per second. Upon entering this state, breathing slows and the body relaxes, which allows access to the imagination. In theta, the mind loses its awareness of the physical body and surroundings, so it eases into a meditative or deep hypnotic state slowing to four to eight waves per second. Finally, delta waves, at up to 4 Hz per second, occur during deep sleep. Carl Jung, the father of analytic psychology, felt the delta state was the bridge to the collective unconscious.

The physical body cannot maintain the high alert of beta without creating disharmony within the body, which we explored when discussing fight-or-flight. Therefore, our conscious awareness must dip into the alpha, theta, and delta states to allow our body rest. This is why a good night's sleep can be so rejuvenating. Meditation heightens our creativity, because our imagination is more accessible. This exposure to higher consciousness equally fosters an expansion of our intuition, as well as gives us a window into what lies beyond what we think we know. This is not to mention the tremendous benefits a less stressful life approach has upon our overall health and wellness.

With our brain more relaxed, we default to our soul senses and become less aware of our physical body. It is in these moments that our soul can fly.

Out of Body Experiences

When the mind and body fall into a deep sense of relaxation some people have what is called an out of body experience, OOBE, or OBE. An OBE is a disembodied state whereby you are aware that your soul is stepping or rising out of your physical body and moving independently within the physical world. During an OBE, I will be lying down and my physical body will become very heavy and I will feel like I cannot move. At this point, my soul lifts up by sitting up while my body remains lying down. If I start analyzing what is happening, I will snap back into my body. However, if I relax into the experience, I will suddenly be outside my body, beside myself, standing, or floating. I have walked through walls into other rooms or buildings. I have traveled to places I know, as well as locations that are unknown to me. I am always aware of being away from my body, because I know I am still connected to it. You can make decisions, move, and function like you normally do. If I have a conscious or beta-level thought, I will be pulled back to my body. When I was first understanding my intuitive abilities and feeling the spirit world, I traveled out of my body quite frequently. I am now able to request an OBE. I state my intention and have the experience shortly afterward. I will feel the familiar sensations or vibrations shifting around me that indicate my soul is about to go on a journey. Such a fun experience!

When the mind is aware the soul is separating from the physical body, it is called a voluntary out of body experience. In this chapter, we are going to explore a few voluntary OBEs including lucid dreaming, past life regression, shamanic journeys, Akashic records, remote viewing, and near-death experiences.

Lucid Dreaming

Dreams come in all sorts of manifestations. Sometimes our dreams combine all of the remnant thoughts of our day into a bizarre series of events for which we can insert a kind of logic to understand. Other times, our dreams seem fantastical with no linear rhyme or reason. Lucid dreams depart from both aforementioned categories because of the verisimilitude of the experience, since you are aware of yourself within the dream. Just like OBEs, you can make decisions, alter your behavior, and actively participate. The main difference is your soul is not aware of stepping away from the body. Lucid dreams are often the first time we connect with our loved ones after they have died. During this virtual encounter, their souls will seem renewed. They can appear youthful and vibrant, especially after a long illness prior to their death. Lucid dreams are an opportunity for our spiritual loved ones to spend time with us to affirm their survival, but most of all, share their love. These dreams are like vivid living, because our soul senses capture the touch, smell, taste, proximity, or feeling with the same conviction we did when we were with that person during their life.

During one lucid dream, I found myself in a bar waiting to meet my father. I discovered I was holding two tickets to surprise my dad so we could see Frank Sinatra. I was aware that he and I had not seen each other in a while. When he arrived, my father said that he and Frank were already quite good friends, as he performed regularly. My father was not only much younger, but he was the best version of himself. We had a long visit that felt like it lasted for days. When I awoke the next day, I had full recollection of what we discussed and truly felt I had spent time with my dad. In fact, I could still smell his aftershave.

EXPLORING LUCID DREAMS AND VISITATIONS

Many people desperately wish to connect with their loved ones after they die. Since our grief preoccupies the finite self, we may have difficulty accessing the slower brain states of our soul. If we are in beta consciousness, we are not apt to become aware of spirit around us. However, when we sleep, the spirit world sees this as an opportunity. Our loved ones miss us equally, so in sleep, they can visit and remind us of their love and presence.

Should you wish to experience a lucid dream, prior to your sleep, focus upon the loved one you wish to connect with. Perhaps have a journal and write them a note stating your intent and desire to connect with them virtually. Repeat "I have dreamt of you, I am dreaming of you, I will dream of you" as you are falling asleep. Give this at least a month of practice and I promise you will have some sort of validation. Remember, this works for our four-legged pals as well. When the dream begins and you are aware of having it, relax into it. Keep your awareness focused upon what your soul senses are perceiving, as that will keep you connected to that moment.

After you have the dream, please take the time to be grateful. Your spiritual loved ones know what you are going through and want to share their love with you. Thank them for hearing your prayer. You can also ask for validations in the natural world to affirm the dream. Keep track of your experiences by keeping a dream journal next to your bed. Its presence solidifies your intention to have dreams that are worthy of writing down. Dreams can give you insights into the state of your thoughts, as well as allow your souls senses to develop. The spirit world also has used my dreams to give me symbols and signs that then appear in my mediumship sittings. When we sleep we are more open to "downloads" from the spirit world, so listening to the soul conversations within your dreams can enhance how you connect to the spirit world. By keeping track of your dreams, you can witness your soul's evolution.

213

Past Life Regression

As my work as a medium progressed, I began asking deeper questions about the truth of my soul. Who was I before I was born and after I died? Had I lived many lives? What happens in between incarnations? Especially, did who I was before have anything to do with who I am now and the people I have in my life?

In my hypnotherapy studies, I was not drawn to help people stop smoking or lose weight, but what did intrigue me was the access a relaxed brain could have to the universe. Not only did hypnosis offer my mind a respite from my own perpetual mental noise, I began exploring the unlimited access of what lay beyond what I thought I knew. It was like jumping on a magic carpet ride where the destination was unknown, yet what I discovered was always deeply personal and insightful.

Past life regression is like taking a tour bus through time, however, you are the main character in all the stories. You will be alive in another life yet be able to consciously comment about what you are experiencing to your practitioner. When you virtually travel, you have a more expanded ability to explore, because you can look up, down, into things, and all around you. Many times, you may discover you are of the opposite gender. It may feel like you are making up what is happening, but by trusting your soul senses and going with the adventure, it is simply amazing what unfolds. People can encounter family and friends in other lifetimes playing similar or different roles. With your soul feeling, you will be able to feel if someone is familiar even though they may look completely different or be of the opposite sex.

My mediumship helps me greatly in regressions, because I join my client, so we are travel mates. As virtual travel companions, we explore pivotal moments within a life and finish by experiencing their death. For people who have never considered they are eternal, when they witness the death of the body and the release of their soul, it is transformative. It is just like an OBE, but this time, you do not have a need to return to that body. After the body dies, the soul leads the journey. Some souls like to go right back into another life, while others foray into the spirit world. People can encounter guides, pets, loved ones, ancestors, deities, ascended masters, and many communicate much like a medium does with their loved ones in the spirit world. Anytime a treatment includes hypnosis, you will be the one experiencing the journey. I just love it when someone meets a guide, because that should be unearthed personally.

When you decide to dive into your past lives, please research your practitioner. Qualified individuals should be certified hypnotherapists, because moments can arise during your session that requires hypervigilant awareness. Your nervous system will be reacting to moments of the past life and depending on the intensity of your experience, your fight-or-flight mechanisms can be triggered. A trained practitioner knows how to handle this situation so you are taken care of and safe. It is such a fun experience that you deserve the comfort of knowing you are in good hands.

I share the following client story, because it is an illustration not only of the curative potential of the past life regression, but also just how much the spirit world is always trying to help us.

Past Life Regression: A Fool's Journey

Emily was half an hour early to her April Fools' Day appointment. I am sure the minutes she waited in her car must have seemed an eternity. Still, she rang the doorbell 15 minutes early, face flushed, out of breath, as if she had run from her car to the door. I liked her immediately. She gushed with enthusiasm about what a gift it must be to do what I loved and complimented me often on the levels of schooling I had attained. You could tell that somewhere along the way she began cheerleading the lives of others as a faraway prayer for a definitive path of her own.

Emily was discovering the life she had led was one she no longer connected with; in fact, she wondered if she ever had. She dearly loved her three children, but her relationship with her husband was empty, and she longed for something more. Having taken care of people her entire life, the idea of doing something simply for herself seemed beyond her comprehension. Despite her reservations, she had finally confronted her husband, expressed her discontent, and was steadily moving toward her new life: something else. She had no set plan, destination, or direction: a quintessential Fool, celebrating all of the best aspects of that card in the tarot. It signifies a dynamic new path, direction, or sometimes the beginning of the next life chapter with its pitfalls and celebrations.

"What do you believe happens to you when you die?" is one of the questions I ask clients before a soul regression. The answers are as varied as the people themselves. It seems most people have some idea, either based on their upbringing, favorite author, or some experience that has shaped their inner vision. I was caught off guard when Emily candidly remarked, "I don't know." She had no idea of heaven, guides, angels, and although she knew there must be something, she had no predetermined concept. I became intrigued when Emily offered that she did not know how she found me or even why she wanted this session. "It just sounded like fun. Perhaps it was because you and my 19-year-old son have the same first name. I don't know. I don't remember," she said.

We finished setting intentions for our session and ventured down the hall to my office where Emily comfortably relaxed in the zero-gravity chair and our adventure began. Soul journeys are truly divine. I often feel like the tour guide on a magic carpet, whose destination only spirit seems to know.

Emily easily began traveling through time to a past incarnation in Jerusalem. Although she had never traveled to that region of the world, she was certain of her destination. When I had her look down at the new body her soul was occupying in that life, Emily realized she was a young man. "I am 19," she announced with conviction and confidence. "Interesting, I am the same age as my son, Austin." She began describing the weight of the fabric covering her body and the depth of cold she was experiencing. "I am sick, very ill. People are around me. I am dying." It was as if she was watching a movie and describing the action as it unfolded.

What was fascinating about this young boy's life was that Emily's point of entry, the first moment she stepped into this lifetime, was the day of his death. Our soul can be drawn to many memories within a lifetime: birth, partnership, hardship, joy, children, and death. However, this was the singular moment to which her soul connected. Her soul knew with absolute certainty and a calm detachment that she, as this young man, was dying. Emily thoroughly explored each moment until she experienced his death. At this point, she explained she floated out of his physical form. Hovering above his body, she witnessed the reactions of others in the room. A comforting and intoxicating presence appeared around her which gently pushed and pulled her out from the room and away from that life. It led her to a magnificent garden, where two very distinct ladies appeared. Emily informed me their names were Thia and Tilly. She began a dialogue with them, discovering that they were two of her soul guides. I encouraged her to ask them about her current life and the decisions she was facing. With the innocence and trust of a child, she silently asked her guides about her decision to leave her husband. Within seconds, tears fell down her cheeks, affirming the divine confirmation she had received to pursue her soul's desire for self-fulfillment and contentment. Thia and Tilly said, "No matter what." It was liberating for her.

217

Next her soul landed in Egypt, again as a male, but this time, in a life that extended well into middle age. This man had spent his early life planning foreign adventures and great learning far away from his limiting village. However, his family demanded he marry for financial gain. Soon after he married, he found himself deeply unhappy with a demanding wife, children, and suffocating obligations. All his plans of freedom and adventure were now limited to his imagination. The parallels of that past lifetime to Emily's current situation were too similar to ignore.

As our session ended and I brought Emily back from the ethers of time, she was understandably disoriented. She had now personally experienced transitioning out of the physical form, met two of her spiritual guides, and was given a cosmic thumbs-up regarding her current choices. She seemed unaware of the enormity of the session, but I knew in time, she might begin to realize just how much her soul engaged, allowing her spiritual awareness to expand that day. She left grateful, glowing, and at peace. Emily wrote me many times over the next few days about her session, sharing new insights with great enthusiasm and prolific punctuation.

Time passed, and it had been months since I had heard from Emily. I was busy preparing for a tarot class I was teaching when I receive an email from her. She was thrilled to join the class, and I knew her willingness to be open to the unknown would be a significant contribution to our group.

Ironically, the focus of our first class was the Fool card. We spent the night exploring all of the beginnings the Fool card can represent, as well as the unexpected unknowns that are required when taking a leap of faith.

After class, Emily and I finally had a chance to touch base. She told me, "Five days after our session together, my son Austin was killed. He had been involved in an accident and died immediately. That life in Jerusalem was so important for me to experience. The fact that I felt I had gone through what he might have experienced calmed my heart. It was as if I was being led to you, so I would not worry. As a mother, you can get lost in wondering what happened. I know because I experienced it. I feel Austin around me all the time. I am constantly talking to him. He seems to want me to study about all of this, so here I am. I am sure if I hadn't talked with Thia and Tilly about what I was planning to shift in my life, Austin's death would have made me stop and disappear back into my life. But they said 'No matter what,' so here I am."

Both emotional, we hugged a long time before we parted ways. The magic and timing rendered both of us beyond words. We said goodbye and I watched Emily cross the street. As she started her car, she rolled down the window and waved with a childlike enthusiasm, then drove away into the night.

Shamanism and Soul Searching

Shamans are the indigenous mediums. Holding the wisdom and sacred space for their tribes, these medicine carriers have an ability to live equally between both the visible and invisible worlds.

Although I had learned how to construct a hypnosis script to help regress my clients, working with shamanic tools to alter consciousness proved much more effective to me. Deep within our psyche, we are comforted by patterned sound. When we are growing within our mother, we listen to her beating heart and the pulsing of her blood. A rattle can accomplish in a few moments what a script does in minutes because it takes us back to our very beginnings as well as to the advent of the human race.

There is a resurgence of shamanic practitioners offering all sorts of ways to work with your soul. Because they are working with you as a soul, their energy work can be very powerful. Should you wish to reframe a pattern, limited belief, or issue, you may wish to try a soul retrieval. It is believed that when we have a difficult experience that is deeply impactful to our emotions, mind, or body, a part of our soul connects to that moment until such time that we have integrated the gift of that experience. In this way, we may still be connected to that experience because it is still informing our life. Once the experience is truly understood and processed, that portion of our soul releases from that moment in time.

During a soul retrieval or soul search, the shaman journeys into the history of your soul to discover the pivotal or original moment your soul experienced the issue you wish to change. Whether in a past life or within this life, the shaman helps you reframe what transpired by helping you shift how you hold the energy and feeling that connects to that experience. Our finite self often holds us in time because of how we remember what happened in our past. As people go back in time to reexperience the feeling of those moments, many realize how powerfully their finite mind has been framing that experience incorrectly. I have witnessed amazing transformations within these sessions. We often retell the stories of our life because we are seeking resolution. Shamanic work can help you disengage from the drama of your past, which helps you be more present. Beyond empowering, these sessions are really fun. You may shapeshift or become an object, person, animal, or being as a mechanism to help remind you of the power of your soul.

A trained shaman will also be able to help you envision your destiny, create a more conscious and sacred connection to your life by working with nature, as well as expand your soul senses in unique and powerful ways.

Akashic Records

What if every deed, action, intent, thought, event, and feeling we experience throughout time was stored in a cosmic computer? The Akashic records have been referred to throughout history dating back to the Akkadians, Assyrians, Babylonians, as well as other ancient Semitic-speaking cultures that mention celestial tablets containing the history of all humankind. The Bible speaks of a "Book of Life" that records the actions of man and is accessible to all souls destined for heaven. Helena Petrovna Blavatsky, an 18th century Russian mystic who founded the Theosophical Society, referred to the Akashic records as indestructible tablets of the astral light which she observed sensitives could access through their soul senses. She noted these records had a creative potential to influence the past, present, and future.

We owe the most profound and valid research into the Akashic records to Edgar Cayce, Christian mystic and founder of the Association for Research and Enlightenment (A.R.E.). Cayce was known as the sleeping prophet because he would receive a client's name, lie down on his couch, fold his hands over his stomach, and go into a light trance sleep. Once asleep, a guide helped him access his client's subconscious experience contained within the Akashic records. Upon waking, he would download a compendium of applicable insight ranging from health issues, past lives, hereditary patterns, current situations, and their soul's history with remarkable accuracy.

Not only did he gain information regarding the individual soul with whom he was working, but he also obtained profound insights on various subjects including ancient mysteries, astrology, dreams and their interpretation, ESP and psychic phenomena, holistic health, personal empowerment through aligning souls with their life purpose, soul mates, meditation, prayer, Christian philosophy, reincarnation, and deeper truths of oneness!

A great story about Cayce using his visionary insight happened when he was struggling within his career. Instead of giving into the advice of others that he should desist his organization, he chose to venture into the future to foresee if the A.R.E. would exist beyond his lifetime. Once he ascertained his facility would indeed outlive him and continue to offer great insight, he came out of his sleep and continued his work. Thankfully, the A.R.E., a nonprofit organization, proudly sits in Virginia Beach and houses the world's most extensive metaphysical library, including all of the 14,306 readings by Cayce. He is a national treasure, and we are blessed to have the profundity of his wisdom accessible to us at http://www.edgarcayce. org.

Remote Viewing

In the early 1970s, the CIA gained intelligence that the Chinese, Soviets, Germans, Israelis, British, and Czechs were all deeply exploring covert operations performed by psychic spies. In 1972, the US Army gathered an elite group of sensitives operating under the code names of Sun Streak, Grill Flame, and Gondola Wish, to name a few, before arriving upon the name "Stargate Project." The mission of this group was to collect intelligence using psychoenergetics or the ability to access deeper levels of consciousness using a technique called remote viewing. The Defense Intelligence Agency Operations Manual from December 16, 1985 describes remote viewing as "a mental process by which an individual perceives, communicates with, and perturbs characteristics of a designated target, person, or event remote in space and time from that individual. Given a series of numbers that defined a target or a location in space and time, the objective of these remote viewers was to ascertain hostile military movements, track enemy personnel, detect changes in forces and hostile intentions or technologies directed toward friendly missions. Additionally, this unit was to offer intelligence for countermeasures to protect against inherent vulnerabilities to which we might expose ourselves." (Defense Intelligence Agency 1985)

Remote viewing is a useful and potent technique. I have participated in coordinated remote viewing experiments with a large group and the results were awe-inspiring. We were given two sets of four numbers, our target representing the physical location we were to virtually explore. Many were able to draw, sense, or identify aspects of the intended location with incredible precision.

In one of the exercise, my senses were overwhelmed with contradictory impressions: celebration, smoke, a painful and disturbing history, sadness, relief, and separation. I drew barriers and felt chaos while my body shivered with cold and seclusion. It was revealed our target was the Berlin Wall. I had neither seen it nor traveled to Berlin. After the exercise, I researched the visuals and history of that area and was astounded by what I could perceive from simply trusting my senses and surrendering to the process. There is great power in working together as a group. It made me wonder what we could do with remote viewing and envisioning the future potential of world peace.

Remote viewing is an art. It demands an incredible amount of detailed observation and surrender to the unknown. It is a skill that needs deep development, nurturing, and commitment. I found these experiences similar in representation to how the spirit world communicates through flashes of pictures, symbols, overwhelming sensory stimuli, and emotion.

NDEs or Near-Death Experiences

Dr. Raymond Moody coined the term "near-death experience" or NDE in 1975 in his best-selling book *Life After Life*, which has sold over 13 million copies. This original work compared the cases of 150 people who had experienced the sensation of leaving their body, as if dying, but then returning to full consciousness. Dr. Moody gathered his NDE research from patients who were resuscitated after having been pronounced or assumed to be dead, seriously injured or ill persons near death, or from the accounts of souls in the dying process.

People who have NDEs can experience any or all of the following: an inability to capture the totality of their experience in words, a recollection of specific words and conversations said after they died by the living, an awareness of silence and peace, a heightened sense of sound, a journey through a dark tunnel or space, a sensation of being out, above, beside, or away from their physical body, comforting encounters with souls familiar and unknown, a being of light who emanates warmth and love, a life review, a border or barrier not to be crossed, and a conscious return to life, sometimes after being told it is not their time to die.

When I was in Mexico years ago, I went body surfing. One wave caught me off guard and I got pulled underneath the water rather quickly. Within moments, I realized I was in two places at once. I felt part of me above the water, looking down and seeing another me struggling in the surf. I felt I was being pulled and pushed upward and away from the ocean. Right then, I thought, "I don't want my babysitter to worry." The next memory I had, I had washed up onto the shore and my mouth was full of sand. I have no memory of how I got to shore or how much time had passed. Unlike the experience in my bedroom when I was visited by the spirit world when I was five and was two me's, I consider this experience an NDE, because I did not feel connection to my body. The spirit world also relates this very awareness to me in my mediumship sittings. It has led me to know that when we die, we are having an NDE that does not return us to our body.

Should you wish to investigate near-death experiences, please find a local International Association of Near Death Studies (IANDS) group. Each group invites guest speakers and truly seeks to explore what is beyond our physical life. I have loved working these groups and I believe you will find their explorations, speakers, and content thrilling.

There are so many ways you can explore the timelessness of your soul. My suggestions are but a few of the journeys you can embark upon. Remembering who you are beyond your physical body is a rich and expansive adventure. Such explorations have helped me understand my fears, resolve issues with my family, deepen my intuitive abilities, and free-fall into the infinity of our universe.

When we explore time as a soul, we find expansiveness, pure possibility, and timelessness. This wisdom contradicts the knowledge we have gained about time. Our soul teaches us such profound lessons about what is really true. Explore the infinity of you and you will discover you are so much more than you remember and know. The hope of having soul conversations with the spirit world, as well as our own soul, is that you awaken and realize just how unique and powerful your soul truly is. May you fall in love with your own soul and then grace the rest of us with your authenticity and magic!

The Promise of the Soul

We need a renaissance of wonder. We need to renew, in our hearts and in our souls, the deathless dream, the eternal poetry, the perennial sense that life is miracle and magic.

—E. Merrill Root

To have the courage to embark upon the invisible path of the soul is to experience the same undiminished wonder as when we behold a sky full of stars. It is part of our nature to be curious and to ponder our place in the universe. To listen to our soul demands a childlike audacity to imagine, discover, and dream that anything is possible. Your soul is meant to deeply contribute to this world. What you create, how you dance your life, and where you wander is the greatest mystery and adventure you will experience. It is the same intoxication that besieged Michelangelo to free angels from marble, Einstein to translate a dream into the theory of relativity, and Mother Teresa to teach us the healing power of love. You are so much more than your physical body. You are a spark of divine light, a one-of-a-kind miracle, and this world needs your soul. Dream, discover, and unleash all of you. You are the deepest hope of the universe. It has been an honor spending time with your soul. May all of your communications be soul conversations.

Recommendations to Further Your Soul Conversations

Parents, Siblings, and Family Grief Support Organizations

Forever Family Foundation: A nonprofit organization exploring the afterlife through research and education while supporting individuals through grief. http://www.foreverfamilyfoundation.org

Grief Haven: Created by Susan Whitmore to honor her spirit daughter Erika, this nonprofit organization supports individuals and families experiencing grief, while providing powerful tools for personal transformation. http://www.griefhaven.org

Helping Parents Heal is a nonprofit organization open to the spiritual exploration of the afterlife, while offering parent-run personal group settings for parents to process and be supported in their grief journey. http://www.helpingparentsheal.org

National Alliance for Grieving Children is a nonprofit organization that supports children and teens who are grieving and provides education for those who are supporting them through their journey. http://www.childrengrieve.org

Grief Resources

ADEC—The Association for Death Education and Counseling offers continuing education and resources to support loss. There is a profound resource page with websites and organizations that support you in grief, death and dying, and trauma. http://www.adec.org

Soul Searching

IANDS (International Association for Near Death Studies): IANDS is a nonprofit organization that has individual groups meetings all over the world with guest speakers and researchers to initiate conversation about near-death experiences and the afterlife. http://www.iands.org

The Monroe Institute: Exploring deeper dimensions of consciousness, The Monroe Institute was created by Robert A. Monroe. It explores out-of-body experiences and the reach of human consciousness. http://www.monroeinstitute.org

Soul Adventures and Conferences

The Afterlife Conference: This annual conference created by Terri Daniel provides wisdom and support for those dealing with the end of life. It also aims to increase awareness of life beyond the physical body, through a mystical approach to death and bereavement. http://www.afterlifeconference.com

227

Soul-Centered Dying

Final Passages: Created by Jerrigrace Lyons to support a natural and green approach to end-of-life care. Their classes and services prepare and support individuals and the community to help plan, guide, and provide support during environmentally friendly home or family-directed funerals. Jerrigrace also trains individuals to work within their own communities. Educators and volunteers are dedicated to retuning to traditional funeral and burial practices. http://www.finalpassages.org

List of Works Cited
and Consulted

Azeemi, S. T. Y., and S. M. Raza. 2005. "A Critical Analysis of Chromotherapy and Its Scientific Evolution." *Evidence-Based Complementary and Alternative Medicine* 2(4): 481–488.

Beinfield, H., and E. Korngold. 1992. *Between Heaven and Earth: A Guide to Chinese Medicine.* New York: Ballantine Books.

Brennan, B. A. 1993. *Hands of Light: A Guide to Healing Through the Human Energy Field.* New York: Bantam Books.

Brennan, B. A. 1993. *Light Emerging: The Journey of Personal Healing.* New York: Bantam Books.

Clements, D. L. 2015. *Infrared Astronomy—Seeing the Heat: From William Herschel to the Herschel Space Observatory.* Boca Raton, FL: Taylor & Francis.

Dale, C. 2016. *Llewellyn's Complete Book of Chakras: Your Definitive Source of Energy Center Knowledge for Health, Happiness, and Spiritual Evolution.* Woodbury, MN: Llewellyn Worldwide, Ltd.

Dale, C. 2009. *The Subtle Body: An Encyclopedia of Your Energetic Anatomy.* Boulder, CO: Sounds True.

Dale, C. 2013. *The Subtle Body Practice Manual: A Comprehensive Guide to Energy Healing.* Boulder, CO: Sounds True.

Dychtwald, K. 1986. *Bodymind.* New York: Penguin Putnam Inc.

Flint, L. 2000. *Voices in the Dark: My Life as a Medium.* London: Two Worlds Publishing Co Ltd.

Gregg, S. 2011. *The Encyclopedia of Angels, Spirit Guides & Ascended Masters: A Guide to 200 Celestial Beings to Help, Heal, and Assist You in Everyday Life.* Beverly, MA: Fair Winds Press.

Harris, H. 2008. *The Twelve Universal Laws of Success.* Wilmington, NC: Likeskill Instuitute.

Institute of Physics. 2013. "William Hershel and the Discovery of Infra-red Radiation." *Practical Physics.* http://practicalphysics.org.

Karpman, S. 2014. *A Game Free Life: The New Transactional Analysis of Intimacy, Openness, and Happiness.* San Francisco: Drama Triangle Publications.

Karpman, S. 1968. "Fairy Tales and Script Drama Analysis." *Transactional Analysis Bulletin* 7(26): 39–43.

Jelusich, R. 2004. *Eye of the Lotus: Psychology of the Chakras.* Twin Lakes, WI: Lotus Press.

Laderman, G. 1999. *The Sacred Remains: American Attitudes Toward Death, 1799–1883.* New Haven, CT: Yale University Press.

Moody, R. 2001. *Life After Life: The Investigation of a Phenomenon—Survival of Bodily Death.* San Francisco: HarperSanFrancisco.

Morehouse, D. 2011. *Remote Viewing: The Complete User's Manual for Coordinate Remote Viewing.* Boulder, CO: Sounds True.

NASA. 2018. "View PUMAS Example." Practical Uses of Math and Science. https://pumas.jpl.nasa.gov/examples/index.php?id=46.

Ponder, C. 2006. *The Dynamic Laws of Prayer.* Camarillo, CA: DeVorss.

Ritberger, C. 2008. *Healing Happens with Your Help: Understanding the Hidden Meanings Behind Illness.* Carlsbad, CA: Hay House.

Rowan-Robinson, M. 2013. *Night Vision: Exploring the Infrared Universe.* New York: Cambridge University Press.

Tice, P. 2017. *Mental Health Facts & Resources.* Substance Abuse and Mental Health Services Administration. https://www.samhsa.gov/sites/default/files/sites/default/files/mental_health_facts_and_resources_fact_sheet_.pdf.

Singh, R. 2016. *Empowering Your Soul Through Meditation*. Lisle, IL: Radiance Publishers.

Todeschi, K. J. 2015. *Edgar Cayce on Soul Symbolism: Creating Life Seals, Aura Charts, and Understanding the Revelation*. Virginia Beach, VA: Yazdan Publishing.

Todeschi, K. J. 1998. *Edgar Cayce on the Akashic Records: The Book of Life*. Virginia Beach, VA: A.R.E. Press.

Tomkinson, Maurice. 2017. *The Everybodies Guide to the Drama Triangle: Straightforward Strategies to Help Reduce Conflict, Improve Relationships and Create a More Harmonious Life*. Sandbach, England: The Hope Street Centre.

Trozzi, M., and K. Massimini. 1999. *Talking with Children About Loss: Words, Strategies, and Wisdom to Help Children Cope with Death, Divorce, and Other Difficult Times*. New York: Perigee.

Zukav, G. 1989. *The Seat of the Soul*. New York: Simon and Schuster.

Defense Intelligence Agency. 1985. *Sun Streak Operational Manual*. CIA. From December 16, 1985, approved release 8/16/2004. https://www.cia.gov/library/readingroom/docs/CIA-RDP96–00 789R001100020001–7.pdf.

Austyn Wells, GC-C, is a spiritual medium, grief counselor, and "soul gardener" who empowers individuals to create soul-centered lives. She combines intuition and mediumship with shamanism, energy medicine, and sacred ceremony. Wells developed the Divine Spark Cards©, which assist both developing mediums and grief counselors to inspire healing conversations with their clients; as well as the Divine Insight Cards©, which assist anyone who wishes to listen to the wisdom of their soul. She is featured in the book *Seeking Jordan* by Matthew McKay, and in the Amazon book *Trust Within* by Molly Carroll.

Foreword writer **Matthew McKay, PhD,** is a professor at the Wright Institute in Berkeley, CA. He has authored and coauthored numerous books, including *The Relaxation and Stress Reduction Workbook, Self-Esteem, Thoughts and Feelings, When Anger Hurts,* and *ACT on Life Not on Anger.* McKay received his PhD in clinical psychology from the California School of Professional Psychology, and specializes in the cognitive behavioral treatment of anxiety and depression. He lives and works in the greater San Francisco Bay Area.

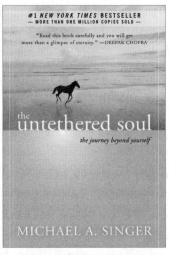